THE HISTORY OF

INFORMATION NETWORKS

How the Flow of Ideas Has Been Used to Build, Change, and Shape the Future

ARNOLD D. STABILE

Disclaimer

This book is intended for informational and educational purposes only. The views and opinions expressed in this book are those of the author and do not necessarily reflect the views of any organizations, institutions, or individuals mentioned.

The author and publisher make no guarantees about the completeness, reliability, or accuracy of the information provided. Readers are encouraged to conduct their own research and consult professionals for specific advice related to the topics discussed in this book.

Any references to historical events, people, or organizations are based on publicly available information and are not intended to defame or harm any individual or group.

The author and publisher shall not be held liable for any damages or losses resulting from the use of this book.

TABLE OF CONTENTS

Prologue

"The most important thing about communication is hearing what isn't said." — Peter Drucker

From the moment humans first etched symbols onto cave walls, we have been driven by a singular, unrelenting need: to share what we know. The flow of ideas—whether through spoken words, written texts, or digital signals—has always been the invisible thread that binds us together. It is how we make sense of the world, how we connect with one another, and how we build the future. This book is about that thread. It is the story of how humans have created, used, and transformed networks of information to shape societies, cultures, and the course of history itself.

Imagine, for a moment, a world without the ability to share ideas. No stories passed down from one generation to the next. No letters sent across oceans. No books, no newspapers, no internet. Without the flow of information, progress would halt. Knowledge would remain locked in the minds of individuals, unable to spread, unable to grow. But that is not the world we live in. Instead, we have built systems—networks—that allow ideas to travel farther and faster than ever before. These networks have been as simple as a messenger on horseback or as complex as the global web of satellites that now encircle our planet. And with each new way of sharing information, humanity has changed.

This book begins with the earliest forms of communication, when our ancestors used pictures and symbols to record their thoughts. It follows the rise of written language, the invention of the printing press, and the creation of postal systems that connected distant lands. It explores how the telegraph and telephone shrank the world, how radio and television brought voices and images into our homes, and how the internet revolutionized everything. Along the way, it examines not just the technologies themselves, but the profound impact they have had on the way we live, think, and interact.

The history of information networks is not just a story of invention; it is a story of power. Those who control the flow of information have always held great influence. Kings and emperors used messengers to maintain their empires. Religious leaders used books to spread their beliefs. Governments and corporations have used radio waves, television screens, and digital platforms to shape public opinion. But information networks are also abilities of resistance. They have been used to challenge authority, to spread revolutionary ideas, and to give a voice to the voiceless. From the pamphlets of the American Revolution to the tweets of modern activists, the flow of information has been a force for both control and change.

Today, we live in a world where information moves at the speed of light. A single idea can travel across the globe in an instant, sparking movements, debates, and innovations. But this unprecedented connectivity also raises new questions. Who decides what information is shared and what is hidden? How do we navigate a world where truth and falsehood can spread with equal ease? And what does the future hold for the networks we have built?

This book does not claim to have all the answers. Instead, it invites you to explore the history of how we got here. By understanding the past, we can better understand the present—and perhaps even glimpse the future. The story of information networks is, in many ways, the story of humanity itself. It is a story of curiosity, creativity, and connection. It is a story of how we have used the flow of ideas to build, change, and shape the world we live in. And it is a story that is far from over.

Chapter 1

What Is Knowledge?

What does it mean to know something? This question has fascinated humanity for thousands of years, shaping the way we think about ourselves, our societies, and the world around us. From ancient philosophers to modern thinkers, the quest to define knowledge has been central to understanding human progress and the role of ideas in shaping our lives.

The story begins with Plato, one of the most influential philosophers in history. In his dialogue Theaetetus, Plato proposed a definition of knowledge that has echoed through centuries: knowledge is "justified true belief." To truly know something, he argued, three conditions must be met. First, the belief must be true—it must correspond to reality. Second, the person must believe it; knowledge cannot exist without conviction. Finally, there must be justification, meaning the belief must be supported by evidence or reason. For example, if someone believes the sun will rise tomorrow, and it does, that belief is true. But without understanding why the sun rises—without justification—it cannot be considered knowledge in the philosophical sense.

Plato's definition was groundbreaking because it introduced the idea that knowledge is not just about having correct beliefs but about understanding why those beliefs are correct. This emphasis on justification laid the foundation for centuries of philosophical inquiry. However, it also raised difficult questions. What counts as justification? How do we know our justifications are reliable? These questions would challenge philosophers for generations.

Aristotle, Plato's student, expanded on these ideas by emphasizing the importance of observation and logic. While Plato focused on abstract, ideal forms, Aristotle believed knowledge came from studying the natural world. He argued that knowledge is built through systematic reasoning and evidence, a process we now recognize as the foundation of science. Aristotle's approach shifted the focus from purely theoretical ideas to practical understanding, influencing how knowledge was pursued in fields like biology, physics, and ethics.

Centuries later, during the Middle Ages, the concept of knowledge became deeply intertwined with religion. Thinkers like Thomas Aquinas sought to reconcile faith and reason, arguing that knowledge could come from both divine revelation and human inquiry. For Aquinas, knowledge was not just about understanding the natural world but also about grasping spiritual truths. This period highlighted the tension between different sources of knowledge—reason, experience, and faith—a debate that continues to this day.

The Enlightenment of the 17th and 18th centuries brought a dramatic shift in how knowledge was understood. Philosophers like René Descartes and John Locke questioned the foundations of human understanding. Descartes famously declared, "I think, therefore I am," emphasizing the role of doubt and reason in the search for certainty. He believed that knowledge must be built on a foundation of absolute certainty, starting with the self-evident truth of one's own existence.

In contrast, Locke argued that knowledge comes from experience. He described the human mind as a "blank slate" at birth, with all knowledge arising from sensory impressions and reflection. This idea, known as empiricism, challenged the notion that certain truths are innate or self-evident. Locke's work laid the groundwork for modern science, which relies on observation and experimentation to build knowledge.

As the Enlightenment progressed, other philosophers like Immanuel Kant sought to bridge the gap between reason and experience. Kant argued that while knowledge begins with experience, the mind plays an active role in organizing and interpreting that experience. He introduced the idea that certain concepts, like space and time, are not learned from the world but are built into the structure of human thought. This perspective reshaped how philosophers understood the relationship between the mind and reality.

In the 20th century, the study of knowledge—known as epistemology—took on new dimensions. Philosophers like Ludwig Wittgenstein and Edmund Gettier challenged traditional definitions of knowledge. Wittgenstein explored how language shapes our understanding of the world, suggesting that what we "know" is often tied to the words and concepts we use. Gettier, on the other hand, famously questioned Plato's definition of knowledge with a series of thought experiments. He showed that a belief could be true and justified but still fail to qualify as knowledge, sparking intense debate among philosophers.

Modern philosophy continues to grapple with these questions, especially in the context of technology and information. In an age where data is abundant but often unreliable, the challenge of defining knowledge has never been more urgent. Philosophers now explore how knowledge is influenced by algorithms, social media, and artificial intelligence, raising new questions about what it means to "know" something in a digital world.

Throughout history, the evolving definitions of knowledge have shaped how humans think about truth, learning, and progress. Plato's idea of justified true belief set the stage for centuries of debate, while thinkers like Aristotle, Descartes, and Locke expanded our understanding of how knowledge is acquired and used. These philosophical explorations remind us that knowledge is not just a collection of facts but a dynamic process of questioning, reasoning, and discovery. It is through this process that humanity has built civilizations, advanced science, and sought meaning in an ever-changing world.

The Role of Knowledge in Human Progress

From the earliest days of human existence, knowledge has been the foundation upon which progress is built. It is the invisible thread that connects generations, the ability that has allowed humanity to adapt, innovate, and thrive in an ever-changing world. Knowledge is not just the accumulation of facts or skills; it is the ability to understand, interpret, and apply information to solve problems, create new possibilities, and shape the future. Without knowledge, humanity would have remained stagnant, unable to rise above the challenges of survival or to build the complex societies we see today.

In the beginning, knowledge was a matter of survival. Early humans relied on their understanding of the natural world to hunt, gather, and protect themselves from predators. They learned which plants were safe to eat, how to track animals, and how to create abilities from stone and wood. This knowledge was not written down but passed orally from one generation to the next, ensuring that each new group of humans could build upon the experiences of those who came before them. This ability to share and preserve knowledge gave humans a significant advantage over other species, allowing them to adapt to different environments and overcome the harsh realities of prehistoric life.

One of the most transformative moments in human history was the Agricultural Revolution, which began around 10,000 years ago. Before this period, humans lived as nomadic hunter-gatherers, constantly moving in search of food. But with the discovery of farming, everything changed. People learned how to cultivate crops and domesticate animals, which provided a stable food supply and allowed them to settle in one place. This shift from a nomadic to a sedentary lifestyle laid the foundation for the first civilizations. Knowledge of agriculture spread across regions, enabling the growth of cities, the development of trade, and the creation of complex social structures. The Agricultural Revolution was not just about food; it was about the power of knowledge to transform the way humans lived and interacted with the world.

As civilizations grew, so did the need to preserve and expand knowledge. Writing systems were invented, such as cuneiform in Mesopotamia and hieroglyphs in Egypt, to record laws, trade transactions, and religious texts. These early records allowed knowledge to be stored and shared across generations, ensuring that important discoveries and ideas were not lost. Libraries, like the famous Library of Alexandria, became centers of learning where scholars could study and exchange ideas. This preservation of knowledge was crucial for the advancement of science, philosophy, and culture.

The Scientific Revolution of the 16th and 17th centuries marked another pivotal moment in human progress. During this period, thinkers like Galileo Galilei, Isaac Newton, and Johannes Kepler challenged traditional beliefs and used observation, experimentation, and reason to uncover the laws of nature. The invention of the printing press by Johannes Gutenberg in the 15th century played a key role in this revolution by making books more accessible and enabling the rapid spread of new ideas. Knowledge was no longer confined to the elite; it became a shared resource that could inspire innovation and drive progress. The discoveries of the Scientific Revolution laid the groundwork for modern science and technology, transforming the way humans understood the world and their place in it.

The Industrial Revolution of the 18th and 19th centuries further demonstrated the power of knowledge to shape human history. Advances in engineering, chemistry, and physics led to the invention of machines that could produce goods on a massive scale. Factories replaced small workshops, and steam engines revolutionized transportation and industry. This period of rapid technological progress was fueled by the accumulation and application of knowledge, which allowed societies to move from agrarian economies to industrial powerhouses. The Industrial Revolution not only improved living standards for many but also highlighted the importance of education and innovation in driving economic and social development.

Throughout history, the sharing of knowledge has been as important as its creation. Societies that prioritized education and the dissemination of ideas were better equipped to adapt to change and overcome challenges. For example, during the Enlightenment, thinkers like Voltaire, Rousseau, and Kant emphasized the value of reason, education, and the free exchange of ideas. Their work inspired political revolutions and social reforms, demonstrating how knowledge could be a force for liberation and progress.

However, the story of knowledge is not just about its triumphs. There have been times when knowledge was suppressed or controlled to maintain power. During the Middle Ages, for instance, access to books and education was limited to a privileged few, and dissenting ideas were often silenced. Yet even in these periods, knowledge found ways to survive, whether through secret societies, underground movements, or the resilience of individuals who refused to let it fade away.

Today, we live in an age where knowledge is more accessible than ever before. The internet has created a global network for the exchange of information, breaking down barriers of distance and time. Yet this abundance of knowledge also comes with challenges, such as misinformation and the need to critically evaluate sources. As we look to the future, it is clear that the preservation and sharing of knowledge will remain essential for addressing the complex problems of our time, from climate change to global inequality.

The role of knowledge in human progress is a testament to our ability to learn, adapt, and innovate. It is the driving force behind every major achievement in history, from the construction of the pyramids to the exploration of space. But knowledge is not static; it must be nurtured, questioned, and shared to remain relevant. As we continue to build on the foundations laid by those who came before us, we must also ensure that future generations have the abilities and opportunities to create a better world. In the words of Isaac Newton, "If I have seen further, it is by standing on the shoulders of giants."

Knowledge is our inheritance, our responsibility, and our greatest hope for the future.

How Ancient Cultures Preserved Wisdom

From the dawn of human civilization, knowledge has been more than just a ability for survival—it has been a sacred inheritance, a treasure to be preserved and passed down through generations. For ancient cultures, knowledge was not merely practical; it was deeply intertwined with their understanding of the world, their spiritual beliefs, and their sense of identity. It was the foundation of their societies, shaping their laws, rituals, and ways of life. To lose this knowledge would have been to lose their connection to the past and their ability to guide the future. As a result, ancient civilizations developed remarkable ways to safeguard the wisdom they held most dear, ensuring that it endured the test of time.

In many ancient cultures, sacred knowledge was closely tied to religion and spirituality. It was often believed that this wisdom came from divine sources—gods, ancestors, or the natural world—and was entrusted to humanity as a gift or responsibility. For example, in Ancient Egypt, knowledge was seen as a divine blessing from the god Thoth, who was considered the patron of writing, wisdom, and science. The Egyptians developed hieroglyphs, a complex system of writing that combined symbols and images, to record their sacred texts, rituals, and historical events. These hieroglyphs were meticulously inscribed on temple walls, tombs, and papyrus scrolls, ensuring that the knowledge of their gods, kings, and cosmology would be preserved for eternity. The "Book of the Dead," a collection of spells and instructions for navigating the afterlife, is one of the most famous examples of how the Egyptians safeguarded their sacred wisdom.

In Ancient India, the preservation of sacred knowledge took a different form. The Vedas, a collection of hymns, prayers, and philosophical teachings, were considered the ultimate source of wisdom and truth. These texts were not written down for centuries; instead, they were preserved through oral tradition. Priests and scholars, known as Brahmins, memorized the Vedas with extraordinary precision, using specific rhythms and intonations to ensure that every word and sound was passed down exactly as it had been received. This oral tradition was not just a method of preservation; it was a sacred act, a way of honoring the divine origin of the knowledge. Even today, the Vedas are recited in the same way they were thousands of years ago, a testament to the enduring power of this ancient method.

Oral traditions were also central to the preservation of knowledge in many Indigenous cultures around the world. For these societies, wisdom was often embedded in stories, songs, and rituals that conveyed important lessons about the natural world, social values, and spiritual beliefs. Among the Indigenous peoples of Australia, for example, the "Dreamtime" stories describe the creation of the world and the laws that govern it. These stories are not just myths; they are a living repository of knowledge, teaching each generation how to live in harmony with the land and its resources. Similarly, in many African cultures, griots—oral historians and storytellers— played a vital role in preserving the history and traditions of their communities. Through their performances, they kept alive the memory of ancestors, the wisdom of elders, and the lessons of the past.

Symbols and rituals were another powerful way that ancient cultures preserved sacred knowledge. In the Mayan civilization of Mesoamerica, for instance, knowledge of astronomy, mathematics, and timekeeping was encoded in their intricate calendar systems and monumental architecture. The Mayans built observatories and temples aligned with celestial events, using these structures to track the movements of the sun, moon, and stars. This knowledge was not just scientific; it was deeply spiritual, guiding their agricultural practices, religious ceremonies, and understanding of the universe. The Mayan glyphs, carved into stone and painted on codices, served as a written record of their sacred knowledge, though much of it was tragically lost during the Spanish conquest.

In many cases, the preservation of sacred knowledge was closely linked to governance and social order. In Mesopotamia, one of the world's earliest civilizations, the Code of Hammurabi was inscribed on a stone stele for all to see. This legal code, which outlined laws and punishments, was not just a practical guide for justice; it was a reflection of the divine will, believed to have been given to King Hammurabi by the god Marduk. By recording these laws in writing, the Mesopotamians ensured that their principles of governance and morality would endure, providing stability and continuity for their society.

The preservation of sacred knowledge was not without its challenges. In many cultures, this wisdom was restricted to a select group of people—priests, scribes, or rulers—who were entrusted with its safekeeping. This exclusivity was often intended to protect the knowledge from misuse or corruption, but it also meant that access to it was limited. For example, in Ancient China, the "I Ching" (Book of Changes) was a sacred text used for divination and philosophical reflection. Its complex system of symbols and interpretations required years of study to master, and its teachings were often reserved for scholars and officials. Similarly, in medieval Europe, the knowledge contained in religious texts and classical works was preserved in monasteries, where monks painstakingly copied manuscripts by hand. While this ensured the survival of these texts, it also meant that they were largely inaccessible to the general population.

Despite these limitations, the efforts of ancient cultures to preserve their sacred knowledge have had a profound and lasting impact. The wisdom of the past continues to inspire and inform the present, providing a foundation for modern science, philosophy, and culture. The hieroglyphs of Egypt, the Vedas of India, the oral traditions of Indigenous peoples, and the codices of the Mayans are not just relics of history; they are living reminders of the human capacity to value, protect, and share what is most important.

In a world that is constantly changing, the preservation of knowledge remains as vital as ever. Just as ancient cultures recognized the importance of safeguarding their wisdom, we too must ensure that the knowledge of our time is preserved for future generations. Whether through books, digital archives, or oral traditions, the act of preserving knowledge is a way of honoring the past, enriching the present, and preparing for the future. As the ancient Greeks believed, knowledge is not just a possession; it is a legacy, a gift that connects us to those who came before and those who will come after.

The Evolution of Knowledge Transmission

For much of human history, knowledge was carried not on paper or stone but in the minds and voices of people. Before the invention of writing, oral traditions were the primary way that societies preserved and shared their wisdom, history, and values. Through stories, songs, and rituals, early humans passed down what they knew from one generation to the next. This method of knowledge transmission was deeply personal and communal, binding people together through shared experiences and collective memory. However, as human societies grew more complex, the limitations of oral traditions became apparent, leading to one of the most transformative innovations in history: the invention of writing.

In early societies, oral traditions were the lifeblood of culture and survival. Knowledge was not written down but spoken, sung, or performed. Elders, storytellers, and spiritual leaders were the keepers of this knowledge, ensuring that it was passed on to younger generations. Stories were used to explain the origins of the world, teach moral lessons, and preserve the history of a community. For example, Indigenous peoples around the world have long relied on oral traditions to convey their understanding of the land, their ancestors, and their spiritual beliefs. These stories were often rich in symbolism and meaning, designed to be memorable so they could be retold accurately.

Songs and rituals also played a crucial role in oral knowledge transmission. In many African cultures, griots—oral historians and musicians—used rhythm and melody to recount genealogies, historical events, and cultural values. Similarly, in ancient Greece, epic poems like Homer's *Iliad* and *Odyssey* were composed and performed orally, preserving the myths and history of the Greek people. These oral traditions were not just about entertainment; they were a way of keeping the past alive and ensuring that important knowledge was not forgotten.

The strength of oral traditions lay in their ability to adapt and evolve. Because they were passed down through performance, they could be tailored to fit the needs of the audience or the context of the time. This flexibility allowed oral traditions to remain relevant and engaging. However, this same adaptability was also a limitation. Over time, stories and knowledge could change, either intentionally or accidentally, as they were retold. Details might be forgotten, altered, or embellished, leading to variations that could distort the original message. Additionally, oral traditions relied heavily on memory, which meant that knowledge could be lost if the keepers of that knowledge passed away without passing it on.

As human societies became larger and more complex, the need for a more reliable and permanent way to preserve knowledge became clear. This need led to one of the most significant milestones in human history: the invention of writing. Writing allowed people to record information in a fixed form, ensuring that it could be preserved accurately over time and shared across great distances. It was a revolutionary step that transformed how humans transmitted knowledge and shaped the development of civilizations.

The earliest known writing system, cuneiform, was developed in Mesopotamia around 3100 BCE. It began as a way to keep track of trade and agricultural records, using simple symbols pressed into clay tablets. Over time, cuneiform evolved into a more sophisticated system capable of recording laws, literature, and religious texts. In Ancient Egypt, hieroglyphs emerged as another early writing system, combining pictorial symbols with phonetic elements to create a versatile and expressive form of communication. Hieroglyphs were used to inscribe everything from royal decrees to sacred texts, such as the "Book of the Dead," which guided the deceased through the afterlife.

The invention of writing had profound effects on human societies. For one, it allowed knowledge to be preserved with far greater accuracy than oral traditions. Written records did not rely on memory or performance, which meant that they could remain unchanged for centuries. This permanence was especially important for laws, religious teachings, and historical accounts, which needed to be consistent and authoritative. Writing also enabled the accumulation of knowledge over time. Scholars could study and build upon the works of their predecessors, leading to advances in science, philosophy, and technology.

Another transformative aspect of writing was its ability to transcend time and space. Oral traditions required a speaker and an audience to be in the same place at the same time. Written records, on the other hand, could be stored, copied, and transported, allowing knowledge to reach people far beyond its point of origin. This ability to share information across distances was crucial for the growth of trade, governance, and cultural exchange. For example, the written laws of Hammurabi in Mesopotamia provided a consistent legal framework for an entire empire, while the written texts of Ancient Greece and Rome laid the foundation for Western philosophy and literature.

The shift from oral to written knowledge transmission was not immediate or universal. For centuries, oral and written traditions coexisted, each serving different purposes. In many cultures, writing was initially reserved for the elite—scribes, priests, and rulers—while oral traditions continued to thrive among the general population. Even today, oral traditions remain an important part of many cultures, complementing written records and providing a dynamic, living connection to the past.

The evolution from oral traditions to written records represents a turning point in human history. It marked the beginning of a new era in which knowledge could be preserved, shared, and expanded in ways that were previously unimaginable. Writing allowed humans to move beyond the limitations of memory and performance, creating a foundation for the development of complex societies, advanced technologies, and global communication. Yet, even as we celebrate the power of writing, it is important to remember the richness and vitality of oral traditions, which continue to remind us of the human voice at the heart of all knowledge. Together, these two forms of transmission have shaped the story of humanity, ensuring that the wisdom of the past can guide us into the future.

Knowledge as a Ability for Survival, Connection, and Innovation

Knowledge has always been humanity's most powerful ability. It is the foundation upon which our survival, relationships, and progress are built. From the earliest days of human existence, knowledge has been the key to overcoming challenges, forming connections, and creating new possibilities. It is not just something we acquire; it is something we use—an ability that allows us to adapt, grow, and innovate. The story of human progress is, at its core, the story of how we have used knowledge to survive, connect, and transform the world around us.

In the beginning, knowledge was a matter of life and death. Early humans lived in a world full of dangers—predators, harsh climates, and scarce resources. To survive, they needed to understand their environment. They learned which plants were safe to eat and which were poisonous, how to track animals for hunting, and how to find water in dry landscapes. This knowledge was not innate; it was gained through observation, trial and error, and experience. For example, early humans discovered how to make fire, a breakthrough that provided warmth, protection, and the ability to cook food. Fire was more than a tool—it was a symbol of how knowledge could transform survival into something more secure and sustainable.

But survival was not just about individual knowledge. Early humans quickly realized that sharing what they knew made them stronger as a group. A single person might learn how to craft a spear, but by teaching others, the entire community could benefit. This sharing of knowledge allowed humans to form stronger social bonds and work together to solve problems. For example, hunting large animals like mammoths required teamwork, strategy, and communication. By pooling their knowledge, early humans could achieve things that no individual could accomplish alone. This ability to share and collaborate became the foundation of human connection and the growth of communities.

As humans began to live in larger groups, the sharing of knowledge became even more important. It was no longer just about survival—it was about building a shared identity and culture. Stories, songs, and rituals were used to pass down knowledge from one generation to the next, ensuring that the wisdom of the past was not lost. This collective knowledge helped communities grow and thrive, creating a sense of belonging and purpose. For example, Indigenous peoples around the world have long used oral traditions to teach their children about the land, their ancestors, and their values. These traditions are not just about survival; they are about connection—about understanding who we are and how we fit into the world.

While knowledge helped humans survive and connect, it also became the driving force behind innovation. Throughout history, humans have used knowledge to solve problems and create new technologies that improve their lives. One of the earliest examples of this is the development of agriculture. Around 10,000 years ago, humans discovered how to cultivate crops and domesticate animals, transforming their way of life. Instead of relying solely on hunting and gathering, they could now produce their own food. This innovation led to the growth of permanent settlements, the rise of civilizations, and the development of trade and governance. Agriculture was not just a technological breakthrough; it was a testament to the power of knowledge to reshape the world.

Another example of knowledge-driven innovation is the invention of the wheel. While it may seem simple today, the wheel was a revolutionary idea that changed how humans transported goods and traveled. It allowed for the creation of carts and wagons, making it easier to move heavy loads and connect distant communities. The wheel is a perfect example of how knowledge builds upon itself—how one idea can lead to countless others. Without the wheel, there would be no modern transportation, no cars, no airplanes. Every innovation is a step forward, made possible by the knowledge that came before it.

As time went on, knowledge continued to drive humanity forward. The discovery of electricity in the 18th and 19th centuries is another powerful example. Scientists like Benjamin Franklin, Michael Faraday, and Thomas Edison used their understanding of natural forces to create technologies that transformed the world. Electricity brought light to homes, powered machines, and connected people through telegraphs and telephones. It was a turning point in human history, showing how knowledge could be harnessed to create entirely new ways of living.

What makes knowledge so remarkable is how interconnected its roles in survival, connection, and innovation are. Each aspect reinforces the others. For example, the knowledge needed to survive—like understanding how to grow food—often leads to innovations, such as the development of irrigation systems. These innovations, in turn, strengthen connections between people, as communities work together to build and maintain them. Similarly, the sharing of knowledge within a community not only helps individuals survive but also fosters creativity and collaboration, leading to new ideas and solutions.

Even today, knowledge remains the foundation of human progress. In the modern world, we face challenges like climate change, global pandemics, and technological inequality. To overcome these challenges, we must rely on the same principles that have guided humanity for thousands of years: the ability to learn, share, and innovate. Just as early humans used their knowledge to adapt to their environment, we must use ours to create a sustainable and equitable future.

Chapter 2

How Stories Brought People Together

Storytelling is as old as humanity itself. Long before the written word, before cities and civilizations, humans told stories. It was through storytelling that early humans made sense of their world, shared vital knowledge, and built the connections that allowed them to survive and thrive. At its core, storytelling began as a fundamental human activity, rooted in the need to navigate a dangerous and unpredictable environment while fostering bonds within communities. It was not just a way to communicate—it was a way to live, to connect, and to create meaning.

In the earliest days of human existence, survival depended on knowledge. Early humans lived in a world filled with threats: predators, harsh weather, and scarce resources. To survive, they needed to understand their environment and share that understanding with others. Storytelling became a way to pass on this critical information. Around the fire, elders might recount tales of successful hunts, describing where to find game, how to track animals, and which plants were safe to eat. These stories were not just entertainment; they were survival guides, teaching the next generation how to navigate the challenges of their world.

For example, a story about a hunter who ventured too close to a lion's den might serve as a warning to others, teaching them to avoid similar dangers. Another story might describe how a group worked together to bring down a large animal, emphasizing the importance of cooperation and strategy. These early stories were practical, but they were also memorable. By embedding lessons in narratives, early humans ensured that important knowledge was not forgotten. A simple list of facts might be hard to remember, but a story with characters, emotions, and a clear outcome could stick in the mind for years.

But storytelling was not just about survival—it was also about connection. Humans are social creatures, and storytelling became a way to bring people together. Around the fire, in the safety of the group, stories created a shared experience. They gave people a sense of belonging, a feeling that they were part of something larger than themselves. Through storytelling, early humans could express their fears, hopes, and dreams, creating bonds that strengthened their communities.

Cave paintings, some of the earliest forms of storytelling, offer a glimpse into this ancient practice. Found in places like Lascaux in France and Altamira in Spain, these paintings depict animals, hunts, and mysterious symbols. While we can only guess at their exact meaning, it is clear that they were a way for early humans to communicate and preserve their experiences. Perhaps they were used to teach hunting techniques or to honor the animals that provided food and clothing. Whatever their purpose, these paintings show that storytelling was already deeply ingrained in human culture tens of thousands of years ago.

As humans evolved, so did their stories. Over time, storytelling became more than just a way to share practical knowledge—it became a way to pass down values, traditions, and beliefs. Oral traditions emerged, with stories being told and retold across generations. These stories often took the form of myths and legends, explaining the origins of the world, the forces of nature, and the rules of society. For example, many Indigenous cultures have creation stories that describe how the world came to be and humanity's place within it. These stories were not just explanations; they were a way of teaching people how to live, how to respect the land, and how to treat one another.

Storytelling also fostered empathy and understanding. By hearing someone else's story, people could step into their shoes, experiencing their joys and struggles. This ability to see the world through another's eyes helped to build trust and cooperation within communities. For example, a story about a hero who sacrificed themselves for the good of the group might inspire others to act selflessly. A tale of a trickster who caused trouble might serve as a warning against selfishness or deceit. Through storytelling, people could explore complex emotions and moral dilemmas, learning not just how to survive but how to live together.

The power of storytelling to connect people extended beyond individual communities. As humans began to travel and trade, they shared their stories with others, spreading knowledge and ideas across cultures. A story told in one village might inspire a similar tale in another, creating a web of shared narratives that spanned great distances. This exchange of stories helped to build bridges between different groups, fostering understanding and collaboration.

Even today, the origins of storytelling can be seen in the way we communicate and connect. Modern stories—whether told through books, movies, or conversations—still serve the same fundamental purposes as those of our ancestors. They teach us, inspire us, and bring us together. They remind us of our shared humanity and our ability to overcome challenges through cooperation and creativity.

Oral Traditions Across Cultures

Oral traditions have been the lifeblood of cultures across the world for thousands of years. Long before the invention of writing, people relied on the spoken word to preserve their history, teach important lessons, and pass down their values. These traditions were more than just a way to share information—they were a way to keep a culture alive, to ensure that its identity, wisdom, and spirit endured across generations. Through storytelling, songs, proverbs, and rituals, oral traditions became a powerful ability for teaching, connecting, and uniting communities.

At their core, oral traditions were about continuity. They allowed people to pass down knowledge in a way that was accessible to everyone, regardless of whether they could read or write. Elders, storytellers, and spiritual leaders became the keepers of this knowledge, ensuring that it was shared with younger generations. These traditions were not just about facts or events; they were about meaning. They taught people how to live, how to treat one another, and how to understand their place in the world. In this way, oral traditions were as much about values and identity as they were about history.

One of the most striking examples of oral traditions can be found in West Africa, where griots—oral historians, poets, and musicians—have played a central role in preserving the history and culture of their communities. Griots are more than storytellers; they are living archives, carrying the memories of their people in their minds and voices. Through epic tales, genealogies, and songs, griots recount the deeds of ancestors, the rise and fall of kingdoms, and the lessons learned from the past. For example, the *Epic of Sundiata*, which tells the story of the founding of the Mali Empire, has been passed down orally for centuries, preserving not only the history of a great leader but also the values of courage, perseverance, and unity.

In the Americas, Indigenous peoples have long relied on oral traditions to preserve their histories, spiritual beliefs, and cultural practices. These traditions often take the form of stories that explain the origins of the world, the forces of nature, and the relationships between humans and the environment. For example, the Haudenosaunee (Iroquois) Confederacy has an oral tradition known as the Great Law of Peace, which recounts how their people came together to form a united and harmonious society. This story is not just a historical account; it is a guide for governance and a reminder of the values of peace, cooperation, and respect.

Oral traditions also played a vital role in ancient Greece and India, where epic poems like Homer's *Iliad* and *Odyssey* and the Indian *Mahabharata* and *Ramayana* were composed and performed orally long before they were written down. These epics were more than just entertainment; they were a way of teaching moral lessons, exploring human nature, and reinforcing cultural identity. For example, the *Mahabharata* contains stories that address complex ethical dilemmas, such as the conflict between duty and personal desire, while the *Odyssey* explores themes of loyalty, perseverance, and the importance of home. These stories were recited by skilled performers who used rhythm, repetition, and vivid imagery to make them memorable and impactful.

Proverbs and sayings are another important aspect of oral traditions. Across cultures, proverbs have been used to convey wisdom in a concise and memorable way. In African cultures, for instance, proverbs like "It takes a village to raise a child" encapsulate values of community and collective responsibility. In Chinese culture, proverbs such as "A journey of a thousand miles begins with a single step" emphasize patience and perseverance. These short, powerful phrases are easy to remember and pass on, making them an effective way to teach values and guide behavior.

Rituals and ceremonies also play a key role in oral traditions. In many cultures, important events like births, marriages, and harvests are marked by rituals that include songs, chants, and stories. These rituals are not just celebrations; they are a way of reinforcing shared values and connecting people to their cultural heritage. For example, in Polynesian cultures, oral traditions are often woven into ceremonies that honor ancestors and the natural world, creating a sense of continuity and belonging.

One of the most remarkable aspects of oral traditions is their ability to adapt and evolve while still preserving the essence of a culture. Because they are passed down through performance, oral traditions can be tailored to fit the needs of the audience or the context of the time. This flexibility has allowed them to remain relevant and meaningful, even in the face of change. At the same time, oral traditions require active participation. They are not static records; they are living practices that depend on the memory, creativity, and commitment of the people who carry them forward.

Oral traditions have also been a unifying force, fostering a sense of belonging and social cohesion. By sharing stories, songs, and rituals, people create a shared experience that strengthens their bonds and reinforces their identity as a community. This is especially important in societies without written records, where oral traditions serve as the primary way of preserving and transmitting cultural heritage. Even in modern times, oral traditions continue to play a vital role in many communities, reminding us of the power of the spoken word to connect, inspire, and sustain.

Epic Tales and Shared Values

Epic tales have always been more than just stories. They are the mirrors of the societies that created them, reflecting their values, beliefs, and aspirations. From the ancient world of Greece to the medieval courts of Europe, epic tales served as a powerful medium for transmitting shared values, preserving cultural identity, and teaching moral lessons. These stories, filled with larger-than-life heroes, grand adventures, and timeless struggles, were not only a source of entertainment but also a way to inspire, educate, and unite people across generations.

In ancient Greece, epic tales like *The Iliad* and *The Odyssey* by Homer were central to the cultural and moral fabric of society. These stories were recited by bards and passed down orally long before they were written down, ensuring that their lessons reached a wide audience. *The Iliad* tells the story of the Trojan War, focusing on themes of heroism, honor, and the consequences of pride. At its heart is the character of Achilles, a warrior whose strength and bravery are unmatched but whose anger and hubris lead to tragedy. Through Achilles' journey, the Greeks explored the complexities of human nature, the importance of self-control, and the cost of personal glory.

Similarly, *The Odyssey* follows the adventures of Odysseus as he struggles to return home after the Trojan War. His journey is filled with challenges that test his intelligence, resilience, and loyalty. Odysseus is not just a hero because of his strength; he is a hero because of his cleverness and determination. The story emphasizes the values of perseverance, family, and the longing for home, which resonated deeply with the Greek people. These epics were not just tales of individual heroes—they were reflections of the collective values of Greek society, teaching lessons about courage, loyalty, and the human condition.

The influence of these Greek epics extended far beyond their time, shaping the storytelling traditions of later cultures. In medieval Europe, epic tales took on new forms, reflecting the values and challenges of a different era. Stories like *Beowulf*, *The Song of Roland*, and the Arthurian legends became the cornerstones of medieval literature, embodying the ideals of chivalry, loyalty, and faith that defined the period.

Beowulf, one of the oldest surviving works of English literature, tells the story of a hero who battles monsters and dragons to protect his people. Beowulf's bravery and selflessness are celebrated, but the story also explores the inevitability of death and the fleeting nature of human achievements. Through Beowulf's deeds, the tale reinforces the values of courage, honor, and the responsibility of leaders to protect their communities. At the same time, it reflects the tension between pagan traditions and the growing influence of Christianity, showing how epic tales could adapt to changing cultural landscapes.

In France, *The Song of Roland* became a defining epic of the medieval period. Based on the historical Battle of Roncevaux Pass, the story celebrates the loyalty and sacrifice of Roland, a knight who dies defending his king and his faith. The tale is filled with themes of fealty, religious devotion, and the struggle between good and evil, reflecting the values of a society deeply shaped by feudalism and the Crusades. Roland's unwavering loyalty to his king and his willingness to die for his beliefs made him an idealized figure of medieval chivalry, inspiring knights and nobles to uphold similar virtues.

The Arthurian legends, which originated in Britain and spread across Europe, offered a rich tapestry of stories about King Arthur, the Knights of the Round Table, and the quest for the Holy Grail. These tales combined elements of history, myth, and romance, creating a world where ideals of chivalry, justice, and honor were brought to life. Characters like Sir Lancelot, Sir Gawain, and Queen Guinevere embodied the complexities of human relationships, exploring themes of love, betrayal, and redemption. The Arthurian legends were not just stories of adventure; they were moral guides, teaching lessons about leadership, loyalty, and the pursuit of a higher purpose.

While the epic traditions of ancient Greece and medieval Europe were shaped by different cultural contexts, they shared a common purpose: to inspire and unite their audiences by reflecting the values and ideals of their societies. Both traditions used larger-than-life heroes to explore universal themes, such as the struggle between good and evil, the importance of loyalty, and the search for meaning in a chaotic world. However, there were also key differences. Greek epics often focused on individual heroism and the tension between personal desires and societal expectations, while medieval epics emphasized collective values, such as loyalty to one's lord, devotion to God, and the responsibilities of knighthood.

Despite these differences, both traditions understood the power of storytelling to shape identity and foster a sense of belonging. Epic tales were not just entertainment; they were a way of preserving history, teaching moral lessons, and reinforcing the shared values that held societies together. They reminded people of their past, inspired them to strive for greatness, and provided a sense of continuity in an ever-changing world.

Storytelling as a Ability for Empathy and Social Change

Storytelling has always been one of humanity's most powerful abilities. It is through stories that we connect, understand, and empathize with one another. Stories allow us to step into someone else's world, to see life through their eyes, and to feel their joys, fears, and struggles. This ability to evoke empathy is what makes storytelling such a transformative force. Throughout history, stories have not only helped us understand each other better but have also challenged societal norms, inspired movements, and driven meaningful social change.

At its heart, storytelling is about connection. When we hear a story, we are transported into the experiences of others. We feel their emotions, understand their challenges, and see the world from their perspective. This ability to create empathy is what makes storytelling so unique. It breaks down barriers, allowing us to relate to people who may seem very different from us. For example, a story about a family struggling with poverty can help someone who has never experienced hardship understand the pain and resilience of those who live it every day. By making the unfamiliar familiar, storytelling builds bridges between people and fosters compassion.

This power of storytelling to evoke empathy has been used throughout history to challenge injustice and inspire change. One of the most famous examples is Harriet Beecher Stowe's novel *Uncle Tom's Cabin*. Published in 1852, the book told the story of enslaved people in the United States, exposing the brutal realities of slavery to readers who may have been unaware or indifferent. Through its vivid characters and emotional narrative, the book humanized the plight of enslaved individuals and stirred the conscience of a nation. It is said that when President Abraham Lincoln met Stowe, he referred to her as "the little lady who started this great war," highlighting the role her story played in galvanizing the abolitionist movement.

Storytelling has also been a vital ability for marginalized communities to preserve their struggles, dreams, and identities. In many cultures, oral storytelling traditions have been used to pass down histories and experiences that might otherwise have been erased or forgotten. For example, during the era of slavery in the United States, enslaved people used songs and stories to share their pain, hope, and resistance. Spirituals like "Go Down, Moses" carried hidden messages of liberation, while folktales about clever tricksters like Br'er Rabbit symbolized the resilience and ingenuity of the oppressed. These stories were not just a way to survive—they were a way to resist, to assert humanity, and to imagine a better future.

In South Africa, storytelling played a crucial role in the fight against apartheid. Writers like Nadine Gordimer and Alan Paton used their novels to expose the injustices of racial segregation, while oral traditions in Black communities kept alive the spirit of resistance. Stories of struggle and triumph were shared in secret gatherings, inspiring people to continue the fight for freedom. These narratives helped to unite communities, sustain hope, and ultimately contribute to the dismantling of an oppressive system.

The ability of storytelling to drive social change is not limited to the past. In modern times, stories continue to be a powerful ability for advocacy and awareness. Books, films, and digital media have become platforms for amplifying voices and addressing issues like inequality, discrimination, and environmental destruction. For example, the novel *The Kite Runner* by Khaled Hosseini brought global attention to the struggles of Afghan refugees, while the film *12 Years a Slave* offered a harrowing portrayal of slavery that reignited conversations about racial injustice. Documentaries like *An Inconvenient Truth* have used storytelling to raise awareness about climate change, turning a complex scientific issue into a personal and urgent call to action.

Digital media has further expanded the reach and impact of storytelling. Social media platforms like Twitter, Instagram, and TikTok have become spaces where individuals can share their stories with the world, often sparking movements and conversations. The #MeToo movement, for instance, began with survivors of sexual harassment and assault sharing their personal experiences online. These stories created a wave of empathy and solidarity, leading to widespread cultural and institutional changes. Similarly, the Black Lives Matter movement has used storytelling—through videos, posts, and art—to highlight the realities of systemic racism and police brutality, mobilizing millions of people around the world to demand justice.

What makes storytelling so effective in driving social change is its ability to make abstract issues personal. Statistics and facts are important, but they often fail to move people in the same way that a story can. A single story about a refugee's journey can evoke more empathy and action than a report filled with numbers. This is because stories engage our emotions, making us care deeply about the people and issues they portray. They remind us that behind every statistic is a human being with hopes, fears, and dreams.

Storytelling also has the power to challenge societal norms and expand our understanding of what is possible. By imagining new worlds and possibilities, stories can inspire us to think differently and envision a better future. For example, science fiction stories like *Star Trek* have explored themes of equality, diversity, and cooperation, inspiring generations to strive for a more inclusive and harmonious world. Similarly, novels like *To Kill a Mockingbird* by Harper Lee have challenged readers to confront their own biases and stand up for justice.

At its core, storytelling is about empathy. It is about seeing the world through someone else's eyes and feeling their joys and sorrows as if they were our own. This empathy is what drives social change, because it makes us care about issues that might not directly affect us. It motivates us to take action, to stand up for others, and to work toward a more just and compassionate world.

Modern Storytelling: From Books to Social Media

Storytelling has always been at the heart of human communication, evolving alongside the abilities and technologies we use to share our experiences. In modern times, storytelling has undergone a remarkable transformation, moving from the pages of books to the screens of digital devices. While books remain a timeless and powerful medium for conveying complex narratives and preserving cultural heritage, the rise of social media has introduced new ways to tell stories—ways that are immediate, interactive, and accessible to people across the globe. This evolution has expanded the reach and impact of storytelling, but it has also brought new challenges, reshaping how we connect, learn, and share in the digital age.

Books have long been one of the most enduring and influential forms of storytelling. They allow authors to craft detailed worlds, explore complex characters, and delve into themes that resonate deeply with readers. A book can transport someone to another time or place, offering an immersive experience that encourages reflection and imagination. For centuries, books have been a way to preserve cultural heritage, pass down knowledge, and inspire change. Works like *To Kill a Mockingbird* by Harper Lee, *1984* by George Orwell, and *Things Fall Apart* by Chinua Achebe have shaped how people think about justice, freedom, and identity. Books give readers the time and space to engage with ideas on a deeper level, making them a powerful medium for storytelling that endures even in the digital age.

However, the way we tell and consume stories has changed dramatically with the rise of digital technology. Social media platforms like Instagram, Twitter, TikTok, and YouTube have revolutionized storytelling, making it more immediate and interactive. Unlike books, which require time and focus, social media allows stories to be shared in real time, often in bite-sized formats that are easy to consume. A single tweet can tell a story in 280 characters, while a TikTok video can capture a moment or idea in under a minute. These platforms have democratized storytelling, giving everyone the ability to share their voice and reach a global audience.

One of the most significant benefits of modern storytelling on social media is its accessibility. In the past, publishing a book or producing a film required resources and connections that were out of reach for most people. Today, anyone with a smartphone and an internet connection can share their story with the world. This has given rise to a diversity of voices that were often excluded from traditional media. For example, activists have used social media to share their experiences and raise awareness about important issues. The #MeToo movement, which began with personal stories shared on Twitter, grew into a global conversation about sexual harassment and assault. Similarly, during the Black Lives Matter protests, videos and posts on platforms like Instagram and TikTok brought attention to systemic racism and police brutality, mobilizing millions of people around the world.

Social media has also made storytelling more interactive. Unlike books, which are a one-way form of communication, digital platforms allow for immediate feedback and engagement. A story shared on Instagram can spark a conversation in the comments, while a YouTube video can inspire viewers to create their own content in response. This interactivity has created a sense of community around storytelling, where people can connect, collaborate, and share their perspectives. For example, during the COVID-19 pandemic, people used platforms like TikTok to share their experiences of lockdown, creating a collective narrative that helped others feel less alone.

Despite its many benefits, modern storytelling on social media also comes with challenges. One of the biggest concerns is the potential for misinformation. Because stories on social media can spread quickly, false or misleading narratives can gain traction before they are fact-checked. This has serious implications for how people understand and respond to important issues. Another challenge is the oversimplification of complex stories. While short videos and posts are engaging, they often lack the depth and nuance of longer forms of storytelling, like books or documentaries. This can lead to a shallow understanding of important topics, where the focus is on quick, emotional reactions rather than thoughtful reflection.

Additionally, the fast-paced nature of social media can make it difficult for stories to have a lasting impact. A viral post might capture attention for a day or two, but it can quickly be forgotten as new content takes its place. This contrasts with books, which have the ability to endure for generations, shaping culture and thought over time. The challenge for modern storytellers is to find ways to balance the immediacy of social media with the depth and longevity of traditional storytelling.

Despite these challenges, modern storytelling continues to shape culture and connect people in profound ways. Social media has given rise to new forms of creativity, from Instagram photo essays to TikTok storytelling trends. It has also made storytelling more inclusive, amplifying voices that were once marginalized. For example, Indigenous creators have used platforms like YouTube and TikTok to share their traditions, histories, and perspectives with a global audience, preserving their cultural heritage in a modern format. Similarly, LGBTQ+ individuals have used social media to tell their stories, fostering understanding and acceptance in communities around the world.

In many ways, the evolution of storytelling from books to social media reflects the changing ways we communicate and connect as a society. While books remain a vital medium for deep, reflective storytelling, social media has opened up new possibilities for sharing stories that are immediate, interactive, and far-reaching. Together, these forms of storytelling complement each other, offering different ways to engage with the world and with one another.

Chapter 3

The Power Of Writing In Changing The World

The Invention of Writing

The invention of writing stands as one of the most transformative achievements in human history. It marked the moment when humanity moved from relying solely on memory and oral traditions to recording knowledge in a permanent, tangible form. Writing allowed people to preserve their thoughts, communicate across time and space, and build the foundations of complex societies. Among the earliest and most influential writing systems were cuneiform, developed by the Sumerians in Mesopotamia, and hieroglyphs, created by the ancient Egyptians. These systems not only revolutionized how information was stored and shared but also shaped the cultural identities of the civilizations that used them.

The origins of writing can be traced back to the practical needs of early societies. As humans transitioned from small, nomadic groups to larger, settled communities, they began to engage in activities that required record-keeping. Trade, for example, became more complex as people exchanged goods over long distances. Farmers needed to track harvests, merchants needed to record transactions, and rulers needed to enforce laws and collect taxes. Oral communication and memory alone were no longer sufficient to manage these growing demands. This need for organization and accountability led to the creation of symbolic systems that could represent information in a consistent and lasting way.

The first known writing system, cuneiform, emerged around 3100 BCE in Mesopotamia, in the region that is now modern-day Iraq. It was developed by the Sumerians, one of the world's earliest civilizations. The word "cuneiform" comes from the Latin word *cuneus*, meaning "wedge," because the writing was made by pressing a wedge-shaped stylus into soft clay tablets. Initially, cuneiform was used for practical purposes, such as recording trade transactions and inventories. For example, a merchant might use cuneiform to document the number of sheep or sacks of grain exchanged in a trade.

Over time, cuneiform evolved into a more sophisticated system capable of expressing complex ideas. It began as a series of pictograms—simple drawings that represented objects or concepts—but gradually developed into a system of abstract symbols that could represent sounds, syllables, and words. This made it possible to write not just lists and numbers but also stories, laws, and religious texts. One of the most famous examples of cuneiform writing is the *Epic of Gilgamesh*, one of the world's oldest known works of literature. This epic poem, inscribed on clay tablets, tells the story of a heroic king and explores themes of friendship, mortality, and the search for meaning.

While cuneiform was developing in Mesopotamia, another remarkable writing system was taking shape in Ancient Egypt. Around 3100 BCE, the Egyptians began using hieroglyphs, a system of writing that combined pictorial symbols with phonetic elements. The word "hieroglyph" comes from the Greek words *hieros* (sacred) and *glyphein* (to carve), reflecting the system's association with religious and ceremonial purposes. Unlike cuneiform, which was primarily written on clay tablets, hieroglyphs were often carved into stone or written on papyrus, a type of paper made from the papyrus plant.

Hieroglyphs were highly versatile, capable of representing sounds, words, and ideas. For example, a single hieroglyph might depict a bird, which could represent the word "bird," the sound associated with the word, or a more abstract concept like "freedom." This flexibility allowed the Egyptians to use hieroglyphs for a wide range of purposes, from recording the deeds of pharaohs on temple walls to writing prayers and spells in the *Book of the Dead*, a collection of texts designed to guide the deceased through the afterlife.

While both cuneiform and hieroglyphs were groundbreaking, they differed in their structure and use. Cuneiform was more abstract and utilitarian, making it well-suited for administrative tasks and the recording of laws, such as the Code of Hammurabi, one of the earliest known legal codes. Hieroglyphs, on the other hand, were deeply tied to Egyptian religion and culture, often used to glorify the gods and commemorate the achievements of rulers. Despite these differences, both systems served the same fundamental purpose: to preserve knowledge and ensure the continuity of their civilizations.

The invention of writing had profound effects on human society. It enabled the creation of complex governments, as rulers could issue written laws and decrees that were consistent and enforceable. It facilitated trade and economic growth by providing a reliable way to record transactions and contracts. It also allowed for the preservation of cultural heritage, as stories, religious beliefs, and historical events could be recorded and passed down through generations. Without writing, much of what we know about ancient civilizations would have been lost to time.

Perhaps most importantly, writing transformed how humans thought about knowledge and communication. It allowed ideas to be shared across vast distances and preserved for future generations, creating a sense of continuity and connection that transcended time and place. The clay tablets of Mesopotamia and the stone carvings of Egypt are not just artifacts; they are windows into the minds and lives of people who lived thousands of years ago.

In many ways, the invention of writing was the beginning of history itself. Before writing, knowledge was passed down orally, and much of it was lost or altered over time. With writing, humans gained the ability to create a permanent record of their achievements, their beliefs, and their stories. This invention laid the foundation for the development of literature, science, philosophy, and countless other fields of human endeavor.

Writing as a Catalyst for Civilization

The invention of writing was one of the most transformative milestones in human history. It was not just a way to record information; it became the foundation upon which civilizations were built. Writing allowed societies to create laws, organize trade, and establish systems of governance that could manage large populations and complex economies. It provided a way to preserve knowledge, enforce accountability, and communicate across time and space. Without writing, the growth of civilizations as we know them would have been impossible. It was the ability that turned scattered communities into organized societies, laying the groundwork for the development of culture, commerce, and government.

One of the most significant ways writing shaped civilization was through the creation and enforcement of laws. Before writing, rules and customs were passed down orally, which made them vulnerable to misinterpretation or manipulation. Writing changed this by providing a permanent and unchanging record of laws that everyone could refer to. One of the earliest and most famous examples of this is the Code of Hammurabi, created around 1750 BCE in Mesopotamia. This set of laws, inscribed on a large stone stele, outlined rules for everything from trade and property disputes to marriage and criminal behavior. It also established clear punishments for breaking these laws, ensuring that justice was consistent and transparent.

The Code of Hammurabi was revolutionary because it introduced the idea that laws should be written down and accessible to the public. This not only provided structure and order to society but also reinforced the idea of fairness. People could no longer claim ignorance of the rules, and rulers could not arbitrarily change them. Writing made laws a shared framework that everyone, from the king to the commoner, was expected to follow. This concept of written laws became a cornerstone of civilization, influencing legal systems in cultures around the world.

Writing also revolutionized trade, which was essential for the growth of early economies. As societies expanded, trade became more complex, involving larger quantities of goods, longer distances, and more participants. Oral agreements were no longer sufficient to manage these transactions. Writing provided a way to document trade deals, inventories, and contracts, ensuring that everyone involved had a clear record of what was agreed upon. For example, in Mesopotamia, merchants used cuneiform tablets to record the quantities of goods they were buying or selling, as well as the terms of their agreements. These records helped to prevent disputes and build trust between trading partners.

The ability to keep written records also allowed for the development of trade networks that spanned vast regions. Merchants could track their inventories, plan their trade routes, and communicate with partners in distant cities. In Ancient Egypt, for instance, writing was used to document the movement of goods along the Nile River, which was the lifeline of the Egyptian economy. Similarly, in the Roman Empire, written records were essential for managing the flow of goods across the empire's extensive road network. Writing made trade more efficient and reliable, enabling the growth of economies and the exchange of ideas and resources between cultures.

Beyond laws and trade, writing became indispensable for governance. As civilizations grew larger, rulers needed a way to manage their territories, communicate with their officials, and maintain control over their populations. Writing provided the solution. In Mesopotamia, scribes recorded taxes, census data, and military orders on clay tablets, creating a system of administration that could handle the complexities of a growing state. In Ancient Egypt, hieroglyphs were used to inscribe royal decrees and document the achievements of pharaohs, ensuring that their authority was recognized and remembered.

Writing also allowed rulers to preserve historical records, which were essential for maintaining continuity and legitimacy. For example, the annals of the Assyrian kings detailed their military campaigns and accomplishments, reinforcing their power and inspiring loyalty among their subjects. In Rome, written records were used to document laws, treaties, and public works, creating a sense of order and stability that helped the empire endure for centuries. Writing enabled governments to function on a scale that would have been impossible without it, providing the abilities needed to organize large populations and complex societies.

The impact of writing on civilization cannot be overstated. It provided a way to create and enforce laws, ensuring fairness and accountability. It revolutionized trade, making it possible to manage complex economies and build networks that connected distant regions. It became the backbone of governance, allowing rulers to administer their territories, communicate with their officials, and preserve their legacies. Writing turned knowledge into a permanent resource, one that could be shared, studied, and built upon by future generations.

Perhaps most importantly, writing allowed civilizations to transcend the limitations of time and space. Oral communication is fleeting, but written words endure. They can be passed down through generations, preserving the wisdom and achievements of the past. They can be sent across great distances, connecting people and ideas in ways that were previously unimaginable. Writing was not just a ability for recording information; it was a catalyst for progress, enabling humanity to build the complex and interconnected world we live in today.

From the clay tablets of Mesopotamia to the papyrus scrolls of Egypt and the legal codes of Rome, writing has been the foundation of civilization. It has allowed us to create systems of law, trade, and governance that have shaped the course of history. It is a reminder of the power of the written word to organize, inspire, and transform. As we continue to write our own stories, we are building on a legacy that began thousands of years ago—a legacy that has made civilization itself possible.

The Role of Writing in Preserving Religious and Cultural Heritage

Writing has been one of humanity's most powerful abilities for preserving religious and cultural heritage. It has allowed societies to safeguard their beliefs, traditions, and histories, ensuring that they are passed down through generations. Without writing, much of what we know about ancient religions, cultural practices, and historical events would have been lost to time. Writing has not only preserved sacred teachings and moral codes but has also helped maintain the identity and continuity of communities, even in the face of change and adversity.

One of the most important roles of writing has been the preservation of religious beliefs and practices. In ancient civilizations, sacred texts were written down to ensure that spiritual teachings and moral codes could be accurately transmitted across generations. For example, in ancient India, the Vedas—some of the oldest known religious texts—were originally passed down orally but were eventually written in Sanskrit to preserve their teachings. These texts contain hymns, rituals, and philosophical ideas that form the foundation of Hinduism. By recording the Vedas in writing, the ancient Indians ensured that their spiritual heritage would endure, even as their society evolved.

Similarly, in Judaism, the Torah was written to document the laws, teachings, and history of the Jewish people. The Torah is not just a religious text; it is a guide for living a moral and meaningful life, deeply intertwined with the identity of the Jewish community. Writing the Torah allowed its teachings to be preserved with precision, ensuring that they could be studied and followed by future generations. This written tradition became a cornerstone of Jewish culture, helping the community maintain its identity even during periods of exile and persecution.

In Islam, the Quran holds a central place as the written word of God, revealed to the Prophet Muhammad. The Quran was carefully recorded and compiled to preserve its teachings, which guide the spiritual and moral lives of Muslims around the world. The act of writing the Quran was seen as a sacred duty, ensuring that its message would remain unchanged and accessible to all believers. Like the Vedas and the Torah, the Quran demonstrates how writing has been essential for preserving religious teachings and fostering a sense of unity and continuity within faith communities.

Beyond religious texts, writing has also played a crucial role in preserving cultural heritage. Myths, folklore, rituals, and historical events have been recorded in writing, allowing societies to maintain a sense of identity and connection to their past. In ancient Greece, for example, the epic poems of Homer—the *Iliad* and the *Odyssey*—were eventually written down after being passed down orally for generations. These works are not just stories of heroism and adventure; they are reflections of Greek values, beliefs, and cultural identity. By recording these epics in writing, the Greeks ensured that their cultural heritage would be preserved and celebrated for centuries.

In the Americas, the Mayan civilization used writing to document their history, rituals, and astronomical knowledge. The Mayans inscribed their hieroglyphic writing on stelae (stone monuments), codices (folded books), and temple walls. These inscriptions recorded important events, such as the reigns of kings and religious ceremonies, providing a glimpse into the spiritual and cultural life of the Mayan people. Even though much of their written heritage was destroyed during the Spanish conquest, the surviving texts remain a testament to the sophistication and richness of Mayan culture.

In medieval Europe, chronicles and manuscripts played a vital role in preserving cultural and historical knowledge. Monks in monasteries meticulously copied religious texts, classical works, and historical records, ensuring that this knowledge was not lost during times of war and instability. These written records became the foundation for the Renaissance, a period of cultural and intellectual revival that drew heavily on the preserved writings of earlier civilizations. Writing allowed medieval societies to maintain a connection to their past while also inspiring new ideas and innovations.

The power of writing to preserve cultural heritage is perhaps most evident in its ability to help societies survive external challenges. When communities faced conquest, migration, or other disruptions, their written records became a way to hold onto their identity and traditions. For example, during the Jewish diaspora, the written Torah and Talmud helped the Jewish people maintain their cultural and religious identity, even as they were scattered across the world. Similarly, the preservation of African oral traditions in written form has allowed the stories, proverbs, and histories of African cultures to endure, even in the face of colonization and the transatlantic slave trade.

Writing has also been a way to bridge the past and the future. By recording their beliefs, traditions, and histories, societies have been able to pass down their heritage to future generations, ensuring that their culture remains alive and relevant. This is why ancient texts like the Vedas, the Torah, and the Quran continue to be studied and revered today. They are not just relics of the past; they are living documents that connect people to their roots and provide guidance for the present.

In addition to preserving heritage, writing has allowed cultures to share their knowledge and traditions with others. The translation of religious and cultural texts has facilitated the exchange of ideas between civilizations, enriching human understanding and fostering mutual respect. For example, the translation of Greek philosophical works into Arabic during the Islamic Golden Age helped preserve and expand upon the knowledge of ancient Greece, which later influenced the European Renaissance. Writing has been a bridge between cultures, enabling the spread of ideas and the growth of human knowledge.

The Printing Press Revolution

The invention of the printing press by Johannes Gutenberg in the 15th century was one of the most transformative events in human history. It revolutionized the way knowledge was shared and accessed, breaking down barriers that had kept information in the hands of a privileged few. By making books and written materials more affordable and widely available, the printing press democratized knowledge, empowering individuals and communities to learn, think critically, and engage with new ideas. This invention marked the beginning of a new era, one in which the flow of information could no longer be controlled by religious or political elites, and it set the stage for some of the most important cultural, intellectual, and social changes in history.

Before the printing press, books were rare and expensive. They were copied by hand, often by monks in monasteries, a process that was slow, labor-intensive, and prone to errors. As a result, only the wealthiest individuals and institutions, such as the Church and royal courts, could afford to own books. Knowledge was concentrated in the hands of a small elite, and access to education and information was limited for the majority of people. This created a world where ideas were tightly controlled, and the spread of new knowledge was slow and restricted.

In the 1440s, Johannes Gutenberg, a German goldsmith and inventor, changed everything. He developed a movable type printing press, a machine that used individual metal letters that could be rearranged and reused to print pages. This innovation made it possible to produce books and other written materials much faster and more efficiently than ever before. Gutenberg's press combined several existing technologies, such as paper and oil-based ink, with his own innovations in movable type and mechanical printing. The result was a machine that could produce hundreds of copies of a book in the time it would have taken scribes to produce just one.

The first major work printed on Gutenberg's press was the Gutenberg Bible, completed around 1455. This beautifully crafted book demonstrated the potential of the printing press to produce high-quality texts on a large scale. More importantly, it marked the beginning of a new era in which books were no longer the exclusive property of the elite. The printing press made books more affordable, which meant that more people could access them. Over time, this led to a dramatic increase in the availability of knowledge and the spread of ideas.

One of the most significant impacts of the printing press was its role in breaking the monopoly of knowledge held by religious and political authorities. Before the printing press, the Church had significant control over the production and distribution of written materials, particularly religious texts. The printing press changed this by allowing ideas to spread quickly and widely, often beyond the control of traditional gatekeepers. For example, during the Protestant Reformation in the 16th century, Martin Luther's writings, including his famous *95 Theses*, were printed and distributed across Europe. This rapid dissemination of ideas challenged the authority of the Catholic Church and sparked a religious revolution that reshaped Europe.

The printing press also played a crucial role in the Renaissance, a period of cultural and intellectual revival that began in Italy in the 14th century and spread across Europe. The Renaissance was fueled by a renewed interest in classical knowledge, art, and science, much of which had been preserved in ancient texts. The printing press made it possible to reproduce and distribute these texts on a large scale, allowing scholars, artists, and thinkers to access and build upon the knowledge of the past. This exchange of ideas led to groundbreaking achievements in fields such as literature, philosophy, and the visual arts.

In addition to its impact on religion and culture, the printing press was a driving force behind the Scientific Revolution. Scientists like

Nicolaus Copernicus, Galileo Galilei, and Isaac Newton relied on the printing press to share their discoveries with a wider audience. For example, Copernicus's *On the Revolutions of the Heavenly Spheres*, which proposed a heliocentric model of the solar system, was printed and distributed across Europe, challenging long-held beliefs about the universe. The printing press allowed scientific ideas to spread quickly, enabling collaboration and debate among scholars. This exchange of knowledge was essential for the development of modern science.

The printing press also contributed to the rise of literacy and education. As books became more affordable and widely available, more people had the opportunity to learn to read and write. This was particularly important for the middle class, which was growing in size and influence during this period. Access to books allowed individuals to educate themselves, opening up new opportunities for personal and professional growth. Over time, the spread of literacy helped to create a more informed and engaged population, laying the foundation for democratic societies.

While the printing press brought many benefits, it also presented new challenges. The rapid spread of information made it more difficult to control the flow of ideas, leading to conflicts and debates. For example, the Reformation sparked religious wars and divisions that lasted for centuries. Additionally, the printing press made it possible to spread not only knowledge but also misinformation and propaganda. These challenges, however, were outweighed by the immense benefits of democratizing knowledge and empowering individuals to think for themselves.

Writing in the Digital Age

The digital age has transformed the way we write, share, and consume information. What was once confined to printed pages and physical books has now expanded into a vast, interconnected web of digital platforms and formats. Writing in the digital age is no longer limited by geography, time, or traditional gatekeepers. It has become a dynamic and accessible medium, allowing individuals to share their ideas instantly and reach audiences across the globe. From blogs to e-books and beyond, the digital revolution has democratized writing, empowering people to express themselves, connect with others, and explore new creative possibilities.

One of the most significant changes brought about by the internet is the rise of blogs. A blog, short for "weblog," is a digital platform where individuals can publish their thoughts, stories, and expertise on virtually any topic. Unlike traditional publishing, which often requires approval from editors or publishers, blogs allow anyone with an internet connection to share their voice with the world. This has made writing more accessible than ever before, giving people from all walks of life the ability to contribute to the global conversation.

Blogs have become a powerful ability for personal expression, journalism, and niche content. For example, a travel enthusiast can document their adventures, sharing tips and stories with readers who share their passion. Similarly, independent journalists can use blogs to report on issues that might be overlooked by mainstream media, offering fresh perspectives and insights. Blogs have also created spaces for niche communities, where people can connect over shared interests, from cooking and fitness to technology and literature. This democratization of writing has not only expanded the diversity of voices in the public sphere but has also fostered a sense of connection and community among readers and writers.

The impact of blogs extends beyond personal expression. They have become a cornerstone of digital marketing and education, with businesses and organizations using them to share valuable information, build trust with their audiences, and establish themselves as thought leaders in their fields. For example, a company might use a blog to provide tips on using their products, while a nonprofit organization might share stories about the impact of their work. Blogs have proven to be a versatile and influential medium, shaping how we communicate and consume information in the digital age.

Another major development in digital writing is the rise of e-books. E-books, or electronic books, are digital versions of traditional books that can be read on devices like e-readers, tablets, and smartphones. They have revolutionized the publishing industry by making books more accessible, affordable, and convenient for readers and writers alike. For readers, e-books offer the ability to carry an entire library in their pocket, access books instantly, and adjust font sizes and lighting to suit their preferences. For writers, e-books have opened up new opportunities to reach audiences without the need for traditional publishers.

Self-publishing platforms like Amazon Kindle Direct Publishing (KDP) and Smashwords have empowered authors to bypass traditional gatekeepers and publish their work directly to readers. This has been particularly transformative for independent writers, who can now share their stories with the world without waiting for approval from a publishing house. Self-publishing also allows authors to retain more control over their work, from pricing and distribution to creative decisions like cover design. As a result, many writers have found success and built loyal audiences through e-books, proving that the digital age has leveled the playing field for aspiring authors.

The affordability of e-books has also made reading more accessible to people around the world. In regions where physical books may be expensive or difficult to obtain, e-books provide a cost-effective alternative. Online marketplaces and digital libraries have further expanded access to literature, education, and knowledge, breaking down barriers that once limited who could read and learn. This has contributed to a global culture of literacy and learning, where anyone with an internet connection can explore new ideas and perspectives.

Beyond blogs and e-books, the digital age has given rise to new and innovative forms of writing. Interactive storytelling, for example, combines traditional narratives with multimedia elements like videos, images, and hyperlinks, creating immersive experiences for readers. Platforms like Wattpad and Medium have become hubs for creative writers, where they can share serialized stories, receive feedback from readers, and collaborate with other writers. These platforms have redefined what it means to be a writer, encouraging experimentation and collaboration in ways that were not possible in the past.

Multimedia integration has also transformed how stories are told. Digital articles often include embedded videos, infographics, and interactive elements that enhance the reader's understanding and engagement. For example, a news article about climate change might include an interactive map showing rising sea levels, allowing readers to explore the data for themselves. This blending of text and multimedia has made writing more dynamic and engaging, appealing to a generation of readers who are accustomed to consuming information in diverse formats.

The use of artificial intelligence (AI) in content creation is another emerging trend in digital writing. AI abilities like ChatGPT and Jasper can assist writers by generating ideas, drafting content, and even editing text. While these abilities are not a replacement for human creativity, they have become valuable aids for writers looking to streamline their workflows and experiment with new approaches. For example, a blogger might use AI to generate topic ideas or create a rough draft, which they can then refine and personalize. As AI technology continues to evolve, it is likely to play an increasingly important role in the future of writing.

Despite these advancements, the digital age has also brought challenges. The sheer volume of content available online can make it difficult for writers to stand out and for readers to find reliable information. Issues like misinformation, plagiarism, and the devaluation of creative work have raised important questions about the ethics and sustainability of digital writing. However, these challenges also present opportunities for writers to innovate, adapt, and find new ways to connect with their audiences.

In conclusion, writing in the digital age has transformed how we create, share, and consume stories. From blogs that democratize publishing to e-books that make literature accessible to all, the digital revolution has opened up new possibilities for writers and readers alike. Emerging trends like interactive storytelling, multimedia integration, and AI-driven content creation continue to push the boundaries of what writing can be. While the digital age has its challenges, it has also empowered individuals to share their voices, connect with others, and explore new frontiers of creativity. Writing, in all its forms, remains a powerful ability for communication, expression, and connection in an ever-changing world.

Chapter 4

The Printing Press And The Spread Of Ideas

The invention of the printing press by Johannes Gutenberg in the 15th century was a turning point in human history, one that transformed the way knowledge was shared and ideas were spread. Before Gutenberg's revolutionary invention, books were painstakingly copied by hand, a process that was slow, expensive, and limited to a small number of people. This meant that books were rare and accessible only to the elite—wealthy individuals, religious institutions, and royal courts. Knowledge was tightly controlled, and the majority of the population had little to no access to written information. Gutenberg's printing press changed all of this, ushering in a new era of mass communication and intellectual growth that would shape the course of history.

To understand the significance of Gutenberg's invention, it is important to consider the context of the time. In the centuries before the printing press, books were produced by scribes who copied texts by hand, often in monasteries. This process could take months or even years for a single book, making books incredibly expensive and rare. For example, a single Bible could cost as much as a small house, putting it far out of reach for ordinary people. As a result, literacy rates were low, and knowledge was concentrated in the hands of a privileged few. The slow production of books also meant that ideas spread at a glacial pace, limiting the exchange of knowledge and innovation.

In the 1440s, Johannes Gutenberg, a German goldsmith and inventor, developed a solution that would revolutionize the production of books. He created a movable type printing press, a machine that used individual metal letters that could be arranged and rearranged to form words and sentences. These letters were then inked and pressed onto paper, allowing for the rapid and consistent reproduction of text. Unlike handwritten manuscripts, which were prone to errors, the printing press produced identical copies, ensuring accuracy and reliability. Gutenberg's press combined several existing technologies, such as paper and oil-based ink, with his own innovations in movable type and mechanical printing. The result was a machine that could produce books faster, cheaper, and in greater quantities than ever before.

The first major work printed on Gutenberg's press was the Gutenberg Bible, completed around 1455. This beautifully crafted book demonstrated the potential of the printing press to produce high-quality texts on a large scale. More importantly, it marked the beginning of a new era in which books were no longer the exclusive property of the elite. The printing press drastically reduced the cost of books, making them more affordable and accessible to a wider audience. Over time, this led to a dramatic increase in literacy rates and the spread of knowledge across Europe.

Gutenberg's invention was a turning point in history because it enabled the mass dissemination of knowledge, breaking down barriers that had previously limited access to information. One of the most significant impacts of the printing press was its role in the Protestant Reformation. In 1517, Martin Luther, a German monk and theologian, wrote his *95 Theses*, a document that criticized the practices of the Catholic Church and called for reform. Thanks to the printing press, Luther's ideas were quickly printed and distributed across Europe, reaching a wide audience in a matter of weeks. This rapid spread of information was unprecedented and played a key role in the success of the Reformation. The printing press allowed ordinary people to read and engage with religious texts, challenging the authority of the Church and sparking a movement that would reshape Christianity.

The printing press also played a central role in the Renaissance, a period of cultural and intellectual revival that began in Italy in the 14th century and spread across Europe. During the Renaissance, there was a renewed interest in the classical knowledge of ancient Greece and Rome. The printing press made it possible to reproduce and distribute classical texts on a large scale, allowing scholars, artists, and thinkers to access and build upon the knowledge of the past. This exchange of ideas fueled advancements in art, science, and philosophy, leading to some of the most significant achievements in human history. For example, the works of Renaissance figures like Leonardo da Vinci and Michelangelo were influenced by the rediscovery of classical texts, which were made widely available through the printing press.

In addition to its impact on religion and culture, the printing press laid the foundation for the Scientific Revolution. Scientists like Nicolaus Copernicus, Galileo Galilei, and Isaac Newton relied on the printing press to share their discoveries with a wider audience. For example, Copernicus's *On the Revolutions of the Heavenly Spheres*, which proposed a heliocentric model of the solar system, was printed and distributed across Europe, challenging long-held beliefs about the universe. The printing press allowed scientific ideas to spread quickly, enabling collaboration and debate among scholars. This exchange of knowledge was essential for the development of modern science and technology.

The printing press also contributed to the rise of literacy and education. As books became more affordable and widely available, more people had the opportunity to learn to read and write. This was particularly important for the middle class, which was growing in size and influence during this period. Access to books allowed individuals to educate themselves, opening up new opportunities for personal and professional growth. Over time, the spread of literacy helped to create a more informed and engaged population, laying the foundation for democratic societies.

The impact of Gutenberg's invention extended far beyond Europe. The printing press eventually spread to other parts of the world, transforming how knowledge was shared and preserved on a global scale. It became a catalyst for cultural exchange, scientific progress, and social change, shaping the modern world in ways that are still felt today.

The Printing Press and the Reformation

The invention of the printing press by Johannes Gutenberg in the 15th century was a revolutionary moment in human history, and its impact on the Protestant Reformation cannot be overstated. The printing press transformed the way ideas were shared, allowing reformers like Martin Luther to challenge the authority of the Catholic Church and spark one of the most significant religious and political upheavals in European history. By enabling the rapid and widespread dissemination of reformist writings, the printing press not only reshaped religious thought but also altered the political landscape of Europe, leading to conflicts, new alliances, and the rise of nation-states.

Before the printing press, the Catholic Church held a near-monopoly on religious knowledge. The Bible was written in Latin, a language understood only by clergy and the educated elite, which meant that ordinary people relied on priests to interpret scripture for them. Books were rare and expensive, as they had to be copied by hand, making access to religious texts and theological debates limited to a small, privileged group. This control over knowledge allowed the Church to maintain its authority and influence over both spiritual and political matters.

The printing press changed everything. In 1517, Martin Luther, a German monk and theologian, wrote his *95 Theses*, a document that criticized the Catholic Church's practices, particularly the sale of indulgences—payments made to the Church in exchange for the forgiveness of sins. Luther's *95 Theses* were initially intended to spark academic debate, but thanks to the printing press, they were quickly reproduced and distributed across Europe. Within weeks, Luther's ideas reached a wide audience, sparking discussions and debates far beyond the walls of the university where he had posted his theses.

The printing press allowed reformers like Luther to communicate their ideas directly to the public, bypassing the Church's control over religious discourse. Pamphlets, sermons, and translations of the Bible were printed in large quantities and in local languages, making them accessible to ordinary people for the first time. Luther's German translation of the Bible, for example, enabled people to read and interpret scripture for themselves, challenging the Church's role as the sole interpreter of God's word. This democratization of knowledge empowered individuals to question religious authority and form their own beliefs, leading to a wave of religious reform movements across Europe.

The impact of the printing press on the Reformation was profound. It not only spread Luther's ideas but also amplified the voices of other reformers, such as John Calvin and Huldrych Zwingli, who called for changes in church practices and theology. The rapid dissemination of these ideas led to the fragmentation of Christendom into various Protestant denominations, such as Lutheranism, Calvinism, and Anglicanism. This religious diversity challenged the Catholic Church's dominance and forever changed the landscape of Christianity.

The Reformation was not just a religious movement; it also had far-reaching political consequences. The spread of reformist ideas fueled tensions between rulers and the Church, as well as between different factions within states. Many rulers saw the Reformation as an opportunity to assert their independence from the Pope and the Catholic Church, which had long wielded significant political power. By aligning themselves with Protestant movements, these rulers could consolidate their authority and reduce the influence of the Church in their territories.

One of the most significant political impacts of the Reformation was the Thirty Years' War (1618–1648), a series of conflicts that began as a religious struggle between Catholics and Protestants but eventually evolved into a broader power struggle between European states. The war devastated much of Central Europe, particularly the Holy Roman Empire, and resulted in millions of deaths. The Peace of Westphalia, which ended the war, marked a turning point in

European history, as it established the principle of state sovereignty and reduced the political power of the Catholic Church. This shift in power dynamics laid the foundation for the modern system of nation-states.

The printing press also played a role in shaping alliances and rivalries during the Reformation. Protestant rulers and communities used printed materials to promote their cause and rally support, while the Catholic Church launched its own counter-reformation efforts, using the printing press to defend its doctrines and attack Protestant ideas. This battle of ideas, fought through pamphlets, books, and sermons, highlighted the power of the printed word to influence public opinion and mobilize people for political and religious causes.

In addition to its role in spreading reformist ideas, the printing press contributed to the rise of literacy and education. As more books and pamphlets became available, more people learned to read, creating a more informed and engaged population. This increase in literacy further empowered individuals to question authority and participate in religious and political debates. The printing press not only transformed how people accessed knowledge but also how they thought about their place in society and their relationship with authority.

The Role of Printed Books in the Enlightenment and Scientific Revolution

The invention of the printing press and the rise of printed books were transformative forces that fueled the intellectual and scientific advancements of the Enlightenment and the Scientific Revolution.

By making knowledge more accessible and affordable, printed books allowed ideas to spread rapidly across Europe and beyond, empowering thinkers, scientists, and philosophers to share their discoveries, challenge established norms, and collaborate across borders. This explosion of knowledge not only reshaped humanity's understanding of the natural world but also inspired profound changes in society, politics, and culture.

Before the printing press, knowledge was confined to handwritten manuscripts, which were expensive, rare, and often locked away in monasteries or the private collections of the elite. The majority of people had little to no access to books, and the spread of ideas was slow and limited. The invention of the printing press by Johannes Gutenberg in the mid-15th century changed this forever. For the first time, books could be mass-produced, making them more affordable and widely available. This democratization of knowledge created a fertile ground for intellectual and scientific progress, as ideas could now reach a much larger audience.

The Scientific Revolution, which began in the 16th century, was one of the first major movements to benefit from the printing press. Scientists and scholars used printed books to publish their findings, share their theories, and engage in debates that transcended national and linguistic boundaries. One of the earliest and most influential works of the Scientific Revolution was Nicolaus Copernicus's *On the Revolutions of the Heavenly Spheres*, published in 1543. In this groundbreaking book, Copernicus proposed a heliocentric model of the universe, arguing that the Earth and other planets revolved around the Sun. This idea challenged the long-held geocentric model endorsed by the Catholic Church, which placed the Earth at the center of the universe.

The printing press played a crucial role in spreading Copernicus's ideas, allowing other scientists to study, critique, and build upon his work. For example, Galileo Galilei, one of the most famous figures of the Scientific Revolution, used the printing press to publish his *Dialogue Concerning the Two Chief World Systems* in 1632. In this book, Galileo defended the heliocentric model and presented evidence from his observations of the heavens, made possible by his improvements to the telescope. The book was written in Italian rather than Latin, making it accessible to a broader audience and sparking widespread debate about humanity's place in the cosmos.

Another monumental work of the Scientific Revolution was Isaac Newton's *Principia Mathematica*, published in 1687. In this book, Newton laid out the laws of motion and universal gravitation, providing a mathematical framework that explained the movements of celestial bodies and objects on Earth. The *Principia* was widely distributed thanks to the printing press, and its influence extended far beyond the scientific community. Newton's ideas became a cornerstone of modern science, inspiring generations of thinkers to explore the natural world through observation, experimentation, and reason.

The printing press not only enabled the publication of groundbreaking scientific works but also fostered a culture of collaboration and communication among scientists. Journals, pamphlets, and letters allowed scholars to share their findings, debate theories, and refine their ideas. This exchange of knowledge was essential for the development of the scientific method, which emphasized evidence-based inquiry and the testing of hypotheses. The printing press created a network of intellectuals who could build on each other's work, accelerating the pace of discovery and innovation.

As the Scientific Revolution laid the foundation for modern science, the Enlightenment, which followed in the 18th century, transformed the way people thought about society, politics, and human rights. The Enlightenment was an intellectual movement that emphasized reason, liberty, and the pursuit of knowledge as the keys to human progress. Printed books and pamphlets were the primary vehicles for spreading Enlightenment ideas, reaching audiences far beyond the salons and universities where they were first discussed.

Philosophers like Voltaire, Jean-Jacques Rousseau, and Immanuel Kant used the power of the printed word to challenge traditional authority and advocate for social and political reform. Voltaire's sharp wit and criticism of religious intolerance were widely read in his essays and letters, while Rousseau's *The Social Contract* argued for the idea of popular sovereignty, inspiring movements for democracy and equality. Kant's essay *What Is Enlightenment?* encouraged individuals to think for themselves and question established norms, encapsulating the spirit of the age.

The accessibility of printed books allowed Enlightenment ideas to reach a diverse audience, including the emerging middle class, who were eager to engage with new ideas about governance, education, and individual rights. This dissemination of knowledge had profound political consequences, inspiring revolutions that reshaped the world. For example, the American Revolution was deeply influenced by Enlightenment principles, as seen in the Declaration of Independence, which drew on ideas about natural rights and the social contract. Similarly, the French Revolution was fueled by the writings of Enlightenment thinkers, who called for liberty, equality, and the overthrow of oppressive regimes.

The printing press also played a key role in creating a public sphere where ideas could be debated and discussed. Coffeehouses, salons, and reading societies became hubs of intellectual activity, where people gathered to read and discuss the latest books, pamphlets, and newspapers. This culture of debate and discussion helped to spread Enlightenment ideals and fostered a sense of shared purpose among those who sought to challenge the status quo.

How Printing Shaped Education and Literacy

The invention of the printing press by Johannes Gutenberg in the 15th century was a transformative moment in human history, and its impact on education and literacy cannot be overstated. Before the printing press, books were rare and expensive, accessible only to the wealthy elite and religious institutions. Knowledge was confined to handwritten manuscripts, which were laboriously copied by scribes, often taking months or even years to produce a single book. This scarcity of books meant that education was a privilege reserved for a small fraction of society, and literacy rates were extremely low. The printing press changed all of this, revolutionizing the way knowledge was shared and making education and literacy accessible to a much broader audience.

The printing press introduced the ability to mass-produce books, drastically reducing their cost and making them widely available. For the first time, ordinary people could afford to own books, and schools and universities could acquire the materials they needed to teach more effectively. This democratization of knowledge marked the beginning of a new era in education, where learning was no longer limited to the elite. The availability of books encouraged more people to learn to read and write, as they now had access to the abilities necessary for self-education and intellectual growth.

One of the most significant contributions of the printing press to education was the standardization of texts. Before the printing press, handwritten manuscripts often contained errors or variations, as scribes would sometimes make mistakes or interpret texts differently. This lack of consistency made it difficult for educators to teach and for students to learn. The printing press solved this problem by producing identical copies of books, ensuring that everyone had access to the same information. This standardization was particularly important for educational materials, such as textbooks, which became essential abilities for teaching and learning.

Printed books also facilitated the creation and dissemination of new types of educational resources. Textbooks, dictionaries, and encyclopedias became widely available, providing students and scholars with the abilities they needed to expand their knowledge. For example, dictionaries helped standardize language and improve communication, while encyclopedias compiled vast amounts of information in an organized and accessible format. These resources not only supported formal education but also encouraged independent learning, as people could now explore subjects on their own.

The spread of printed materials had a profound impact on literacy rates, particularly during the Renaissance and Reformation. The Renaissance, a period of cultural and intellectual revival that began in the 14th century, was fueled by the rediscovery of classical texts and the spread of new ideas. The printing press made it possible to reproduce and distribute these texts on a large scale, allowing more people to engage with literature, philosophy, and science. As books became more accessible, literacy rates began to rise, as individuals sought to read and understand the wealth of knowledge that was now available to them.

The Reformation, which began in the early 16th century, further accelerated the spread of literacy. Religious reformers like Martin Luther emphasized the importance of reading the Bible in one's own language, rather than relying on clergy to interpret it. The printing press made it possible to produce Bibles and other religious texts in vernacular languages, empowering ordinary people to engage with their faith on a personal level. This emphasis on individual reading and interpretation encouraged more people to learn to read, contributing to a significant increase in literacy rates across Europe.

The rise of literacy had far-reaching consequences for society. As more people became literate, they were able to access a wider range of ideas and perspectives, fostering critical thinking and intellectual curiosity. This democratization of knowledge empowered individuals to question authority, challenge traditional beliefs, and seek new solutions to problems. It also laid the foundation for the development of public education systems, as societies recognized the importance of literacy and education for economic and social progress.

The printing press also played a key role in shaping the modern concept of education. With the availability of standardized textbooks and other educational materials, schools and universities were able to develop more structured curricula and reach larger numbers of students. The spread of printed books also encouraged the establishment of libraries, which became centers of learning and intellectual exchange. These developments helped to create a culture of education that valued knowledge and lifelong learning, setting the stage for the modern educational systems we know today.

Chapter 5

The Postal System

The Origins of Postal Systems

The origins of postal systems can be traced back to the need for empires to communicate across vast distances. In the ancient world, where territories stretched over thousands of miles, effective communication was essential for governance, military coordination, and maintaining control over far-flung regions. Two of the most remarkable early postal systems were developed in the Persian Empire and the Roman Empire. These systems not only revolutionized the way messages were delivered but also played a crucial role in uniting empires, fostering trade, and enabling cultural exchange.

The Persian Empire, under the rule of Darius I in the 6th century BCE, established one of the earliest organized postal systems, known as the *Angarium*. This system was designed to ensure the swift and reliable delivery of messages across the vast Persian Empire, which stretched from the Indus Valley in the east to the Aegean Sea in the west. The *Angarium* relied on a network of relay stations, or post houses, strategically placed along the Royal Road, a major highway that spanned over 1,500 miles. Couriers, often mounted on horseback, would carry messages from one station to the next, where fresh horses and riders were waiting to continue the journey.

This relay system allowed messages to travel at remarkable speeds for the time. Herodotus, the ancient Greek historian, marveled at the efficiency of the Persian couriers, noting that "neither snow, nor rain, nor heat, nor gloom of night" could delay their progress. The *Angarium* was a vital ability for the Persian kings, enabling them to send orders, receive reports, and coordinate military campaigns across their vast empire. It also helped maintain control over distant territories by ensuring that the central government could stay informed about events in even the most remote regions.

The Persian postal system was not just a practical innovation; it was a symbol of the empire's power and organization. By creating a reliable communication network, the Persians demonstrated their ability to govern a diverse and sprawling empire. The *Angarium* set a precedent for future postal systems, inspiring other civilizations to develop their own methods of long-distance communication.

Centuries later, the Roman Empire built upon the innovations of the Persians and created an even more sophisticated postal system known as the *Cursus Publicus*. Established during the reign of Emperor Augustus in the 1st century BCE, the *Cursus Publicus* was designed to facilitate the efficient delivery of official messages and documents across the Roman Empire, which at its height spanned three continents. Like the Persian *Angarium*, the Roman system relied on a network of roads, relay stations, and couriers.

The Romans were renowned for their engineering prowess, and their extensive network of roads was a key factor in the success of the *Cursus Publicus*. These roads, built with remarkable precision and durability, connected cities, towns, and military outposts across the empire. Relay stations, known as *mutationes*, were placed at regular intervals along these roads, providing fresh horses and supplies for couriers. Larger stations, called *mansiones*, offered accommodations for travelers and officials. This infrastructure allowed messages to be delivered quickly and efficiently, even over long distances.

The *Cursus Publicus* was primarily used for official purposes, such as delivering orders from the emperor, military dispatches, and tax records. However, it also facilitated trade and cultural exchange by making travel and communication easier for merchants, scholars, and diplomats. The system helped to unify the Roman Empire, creating a sense of connection between its diverse provinces and ensuring that the central government could maintain control over its vast territories.

The efficiency of the *Cursus Publicus* was a testament to the organizational skills of the Romans. Couriers could travel up to 50 miles a day, a remarkable speed for the time, and messages could be sent from one end of the empire to the other in a matter of weeks. This ability to communicate quickly and reliably was essential for the administration of such a large and complex empire. It allowed the Romans to respond to crises, coordinate military campaigns, and enforce laws across their territories.

The Roman postal system also had a significant cultural impact. By connecting distant regions, the *Cursus Publicus* facilitated the exchange of ideas, technologies, and traditions. It helped to spread Roman culture and influence, as well as to integrate the diverse peoples of the empire into a shared political and economic system. The roads and relay stations of the *Cursus Publicus* became arteries of communication and commerce, linking the empire together and ensuring its stability.

The Role of Postal Networks in Trade and Governance

Throughout history, postal networks have been the backbone of communication, playing a vital role in facilitating trade and enabling effective governance across vast territories. These networks, designed to ensure the swift and reliable transmission of messages, were essential for maintaining control over empires, coordinating administrative functions, and fostering economic growth. From the ancient Persian Angarium to the Roman Cursus Publicus and beyond, postal systems have been a testament to the ingenuity of civilizations in overcoming the challenges of distance and time.

The origins of postal networks can be traced back to the Persian Empire under Darius I in the 6th century BCE. The Persian Angarium was one of the earliest organized postal systems, created to ensure that messages could travel quickly across the empire, which stretched from the Indus Valley to the Mediterranean. The Angarium relied on a network of relay stations, where couriers on horseback would pass messages to fresh riders, allowing information to travel at remarkable speeds for the time. This system was crucial for governance, as it enabled the Persian kings to issue decrees, coordinate military campaigns, and maintain control over distant provinces. The Angarium also supported trade by providing merchants with a reliable way to communicate across long distances, exchange information about markets, and coordinate the movement of goods along the empire's trade routes.

The Roman Empire built upon the innovations of the Persians, creating an even more sophisticated postal system known as the Cursus Publicus. Established during the reign of Emperor Augustus in the 1st century BCE, the Cursus Publicus was designed to facilitate the efficient delivery of official messages and documents across the vast Roman Empire. The system relied on an extensive network of roads, relay stations, and couriers, allowing messages to travel quickly and reliably. These roads, some of which are still in use today, connected cities, towns, and military outposts, ensuring that the central government could maintain control over its territories.

The Cursus Publicus was not only a ability for governance but also a catalyst for economic growth. By enabling merchants to communicate with one another and coordinate the movement of goods, the postal network helped to integrate the Roman economy and foster connections between regions. For example, a merchant in Gaul could use the postal system to send a message to a supplier in Egypt, arranging for the shipment of goods such as grain, wine, or textiles. This ability to exchange information and coordinate trade across long distances was essential for the smooth operation of the Roman economy and contributed to the prosperity of the empire.

As empires expanded and economies grew more complex, postal networks evolved to meet the needs of their societies. One of the most remarkable examples of this evolution was the Yam system of the Mongol Empire in the 13th and 14th centuries. The Mongols, under the leadership of Genghis Khan, created a vast postal network that spanned their enormous empire, which stretched from China to Eastern Europe. The Yam system relied on a network of relay stations, where couriers could rest, change horses, and continue their journeys. This system allowed messages to travel up to 200 miles a day, an incredible speed for the time.

The Yam system was essential for governance, as it enabled the Mongol rulers to maintain control over their vast territories, issue orders, and respond to crises in a timely manner. It also supported trade by providing merchants with a reliable way to communicate and coordinate their activities along the Silk Road, the network of trade routes that connected East and West. The Mongol postal network helped to create a more interconnected world, facilitating the exchange of goods, ideas, and technologies between different cultures.

In early modern Europe, postal networks underwent significant reforms to meet the needs of expanding states and economies. For example, in the 16th and 17th centuries, many European countries established state-run postal services to improve communication and support governance. These postal systems were often modeled on earlier networks, such as the Roman Cursus Publicus, but incorporated new technologies and innovations. The introduction of standardized postage rates, for example, made it easier and more affordable for people to send letters and packages, further integrating economies and societies.

Postal networks in early modern Europe also played a crucial role in fostering trade and economic growth. Merchants used the postal system to exchange information about market conditions, negotiate contracts, and coordinate the movement of goods. This ability to communicate quickly and reliably was essential for the development of global trade networks, as it allowed merchants to respond to changes in supply and demand, manage risks, and seize new opportunities. The postal system also supported the growth of financial markets, as it enabled the rapid exchange of information about prices, investments, and credit.

In addition to their economic benefits, postal networks were indispensable for governance. Rulers and administrators relied on the postal system to issue decrees, collect taxes, and maintain order. For example, during the reign of Louis XIV in France, the royal postal service was used to deliver official documents, coordinate military campaigns, and monitor the activities of provincial governors. The ability to communicate quickly and efficiently allowed the central government to maintain control over its territories and respond to challenges as they arose.

The Democratization of Communication

The development of postal systems and the widespread use of letters marked a profound shift in the way people communicated, making it possible for individuals across different social classes to connect with one another over long distances. In earlier times, communication was often a privilege reserved for the elite. Kings, nobles, and scholars had access to messengers and scribes, while the majority of people relied on word of mouth or had no means of long-distance communication at all. However, as postal networks expanded and letter writing became more affordable, communication was democratized, allowing ordinary people to share their thoughts, emotions, and experiences in ways that were previously unimaginable.

The expansion of postal systems, such as the Roman *Cursus Publicus*, the Mongol Yam system, and later the state-run postal services of early modern Europe, played a crucial role in making communication more accessible. These networks, originally designed for official and governmental use, gradually opened up to the public, enabling merchants, travelers, and eventually ordinary citizens to send and receive letters. By the 18th and 19th centuries, postal reforms in many countries, such as the introduction of standardized postage rates and prepaid stamps, made letter writing affordable for people from all walks of life. This accessibility transformed communication, allowing families, friends, and even strangers to maintain connections across great distances.

Letters became a powerful medium for personal expression. Unlike official documents or public proclamations, letters were intimate and personal, written from one individual to another. They allowed people to share their innermost thoughts, emotions, and ideas in a way that felt private and meaningful. For families separated by distance, letters were a lifeline, helping to maintain bonds and provide comfort. A parent could write to a child studying in another city, offering advice and encouragement. A soldier on the battlefield could send a letter home, reassuring loved ones of their safety and sharing their hopes and fears. These exchanges of words created a sense of closeness, even when physical distance made it impossible to be together.

During times of war, letters played an especially important role in maintaining morale. Soldiers and their families relied on correspondence to stay connected, offering each other strength and support in the face of uncertainty and hardship. For example, during World War I and World War II, millions of letters were exchanged between soldiers and their loved ones. These letters were often filled with expressions of love, hope, and longing, providing a sense of normalcy and humanity amidst the chaos of war. For many, the arrival of a letter was a moment of joy and relief, a reminder that they were not alone.

Beyond personal connections, letters also became a means of exchanging knowledge and culture. In the 18th century, during the Enlightenment, letters were a key ability for intellectuals to share ideas and engage in debates. Philosophers like Voltaire, Rousseau, and Diderot used correspondence to discuss topics such as reason, liberty, and human rights, shaping the intellectual movements of their time. These letters were not just private exchanges; they were often shared, published, and circulated, influencing public opinion and inspiring change. The democratization of communication through letters allowed ideas to spread more widely, breaking down barriers between social classes and fostering a sense of shared humanity.

The impact of letter writing extended beyond intellectual circles. Ordinary people used letters to share news, tell stories, and preserve traditions. A farmer might write to a relative in another town, describing the harvest and local events. A young woman might correspond with a friend, sharing her dreams and aspirations. These letters, often written in simple language, captured the everyday lives of people and provided a window into their world. They helped to create a sense of community and connection, even among those who had never met in person.

The democratization of communication through letters also had a profound impact on literacy. As more people began to write and receive letters, the ability to read and write became increasingly important. This demand for literacy encouraged the spread of education, as individuals sought to learn the skills needed to participate in this new form of communication. In this way, letters not only connected people but also contributed to the broader development of society, fostering a culture of learning and self-expression.

Postal Systems in the Age of Industrialization

The Age of Industrialization brought sweeping changes to nearly every aspect of human life, and postal systems were no exception. During the Industrial Revolution, which began in the late 18th century and continued into the 19th century, postal networks evolved and expanded dramatically, transforming communication and connecting people, businesses, and governments on an unprecedented scale. Advancements in transportation, technology, and infrastructure revolutionized the speed, efficiency, and accessibility of postal services, making them a vital part of modern society.

Before industrialization, postal systems were often slow and limited in reach. Messages traveled by horse-drawn carriages or on foot, and the delivery of letters and packages could take weeks or even months, especially over long distances. However, the Industrial Revolution introduced new modes of transportation that revolutionized the way mail was delivered. Railways, for example, became a game-changer for postal services. Trains could carry large quantities of mail at high speeds, connecting cities and towns more efficiently than ever before. A letter that once took days to travel between two locations could now arrive in a matter of hours. Railways also allowed for the establishment of regular and reliable mail schedules, ensuring that people and businesses could depend on timely communication.

Steamships further expanded the reach of postal systems, enabling mail to cross oceans and connect continents. Before the advent of steamships, international mail relied on sailing ships, which were at the mercy of wind and weather. Steamships, powered by engines, were faster and more reliable, reducing the time it took for letters and packages to travel between Europe, the Americas, and other parts of the world. This advancement was particularly important for global trade and diplomacy, as it allowed businesses and governments to communicate more effectively across vast distances.

Industrialization also brought innovations that made postal services more accessible to the general public. One of the most significant developments was the introduction of the postage stamp. In 1840, Britain introduced the Penny Black, the world's first adhesive postage stamp. This small but revolutionary invention simplified the process of sending mail. Before stamps, the cost of sending a letter was often paid by the recipient, and rates varied based on distance and other factors, making the system complicated and inconsistent. The Penny Black introduced a standardized rate, allowing anyone to send a letter anywhere in the country for a single penny. This innovation democratized communication, making it affordable and easy for ordinary people to send and receive mail.

The success of the Penny Black inspired other countries to adopt similar systems. By the mid-19th century, many nations in Europe and North America had introduced postage stamps and standardized rates, transforming their postal networks into efficient and accessible public services. These changes allowed individuals, businesses, and governments to communicate more effectively, fostering economic growth, social cohesion, and global connections.

The expansion of national postal systems during the Age of Industrialization was a testament to the transformative power of industrial progress. In the United States, for example, the establishment of the U.S. Postal Service and the construction of transcontinental railroads in the 19th century created a vast and interconnected postal network. This network not only connected cities and towns but also reached remote rural areas, ensuring that even the most isolated communities could participate in the exchange of information and goods. Similarly, in Europe, countries like France, Germany, and Britain invested heavily in their postal infrastructure, building networks of post offices, rail lines, and delivery routes that brought people and businesses closer together.

The impact of these postal networks on commerce was profound. Businesses relied on the postal system to send invoices, contracts, and orders, enabling them to operate more efficiently and expand their reach. Catalogs and mail-order services became popular, allowing consumers to purchase goods from distant suppliers and have them delivered to their doorsteps. This new way of doing business not only boosted economic activity but also laid the groundwork for modern e-commerce.

Postal systems also played a crucial role in the spread of ideas and information. Newspapers, magazines, and books could now be distributed quickly and widely, reaching audiences that had previously been out of reach. This dissemination of knowledge fueled intellectual and cultural movements, from the Enlightenment to the rise of mass education. People could stay informed about current events, learn about new technologies, and engage with the ideas of thinkers and writers from around the world. The postal system became a bridge between cultures, fostering a sense of global interconnectedness.

On a personal level, the expansion of postal services strengthened relationships and brought people closer together. Families separated by distance could stay in touch through letters, sharing news, emotions, and experiences. Immigrants who had moved to new countries could maintain connections with their loved ones back home, easing the pain of separation and creating a sense of continuity in their lives. The ability to communicate across distances helped to build and sustain personal and professional relationships, making the world feel smaller and more connected.

Chapter 6

The Telegraph And Telephone

The Telegraph

The invention of the telegraph in the 19th century marked a revolutionary moment in human history, transforming communication in ways that were previously unimaginable. For the first time, messages could be sent almost instantly over long distances, replacing the slower methods of letters, messengers, and postal systems. The telegraph was not just a technological breakthrough; it was the foundation of modern communication networks, ushering in a new era of global connectivity and real-time information exchange.

The development of the telegraph was the result of years of experimentation and innovation in the field of electricity. Early attempts to create a system for transmitting messages electrically began in the late 18th century, but it wasn't until the 1830s and 1840s that the telegraph as we know it began to take shape. Samuel Morse, an American inventor and artist, played a pivotal role in this process. Working alongside Alfred Vail and Leonard Gale, Morse developed a practical and reliable telegraph system that used electrical signals to transmit messages over wires. To make this system work, Morse also created a code—later known as Morse code—that assigned dots and dashes to letters and numbers, allowing messages to be encoded and decoded quickly and efficiently.

The first successful demonstration of Morse's telegraph system took place in 1844, when a message was sent from Washington, D.C., to Baltimore, Maryland. The message, "What hath God wrought," was a biblical phrase that captured the awe and significance of this groundbreaking achievement. This demonstration proved that the telegraph could transmit messages over long distances almost instantaneously, paving the way for its widespread adoption.

The telegraph revolutionized communication by replacing slower, more labor-intensive methods with a system that allowed for real-time information exchange. Before the telegraph, messages had to be physically carried by messengers, ships, or postal services, which could take days, weeks, or even months to reach their destination. The telegraph eliminated these delays, enabling people to send and receive messages in a matter of minutes. This newfound speed had a profound impact on society, transforming commerce, governance, journalism, and everyday life.

In the world of commerce, the telegraph became an indispensable ability for businesses. Merchants and traders used it to coordinate the movement of goods, negotiate prices, and stay informed about market conditions. For example, stock exchanges relied on the telegraph to transmit financial data, allowing investors to make decisions based on up-to-date information. The telegraph also played a crucial role in the development of railroads, as it allowed railway companies to manage schedules, prevent accidents, and communicate with stations along their routes. By enabling businesses to operate more efficiently and respond to changes in real time, the telegraph contributed to the rapid growth of industrial economies.

Governments, too, quickly recognized the value of the telegraph for military and administrative purposes. During times of war, the telegraph allowed commanders to issue orders, gather intelligence, and coordinate troop movements with unprecedented speed. For example, during the American Civil War, both the Union and Confederate armies used the telegraph to communicate across vast battlefields, giving them a strategic advantage. In peacetime, governments used the telegraph to manage their territories, collect taxes, and respond to crises. The ability to transmit information instantly helped centralize authority and improve the efficiency of governance.

The telegraph also transformed journalism, ushering in the era of real-time news reporting. Before the telegraph, news often traveled slowly, arriving days or weeks after an event had occurred. With the telegraph, reporters could send updates from the field almost immediately, allowing newspapers to publish breaking news stories. This innovation changed the way people consumed information, creating a more informed and connected public. One notable example of the telegraph's impact on journalism was its role in reporting the Crimean War (1853–1856), where correspondents used the telegraph to send updates directly from the battlefield, giving readers a sense of immediacy and urgency.

The global significance of the telegraph became even more apparent with the construction of the first transatlantic telegraph cable in 1858. This ambitious project connected Europe and North America, allowing messages to be sent across the Atlantic Ocean in a matter of minutes. Although the first cable failed after a few weeks, subsequent efforts succeeded, and by 1866, a permanent transatlantic cable was in place. This achievement marked the beginning of global communication networks, shrinking the world and fostering international trade, diplomacy, and cultural exchange.

The telegraph's impact on society was profound. It not only revolutionized the way people communicated but also changed how they thought about time and distance. For the first time in history, information could travel faster than people or goods, creating a sense of immediacy and interconnectedness that reshaped the modern world. The telegraph also laid the groundwork for future innovations in communication, such as the telephone, radio, and eventually the internet. By demonstrating the power of instant communication, the telegraph set the stage for the digital age we live in today.

How the Telegraph Revolutionized Business, War, and Journalism

The invention of the telegraph in the 19th century revolutionized the way people communicated, transforming not only personal correspondence but also the critical areas of business, war, and journalism. By enabling messages to be transmitted almost instantly over long distances, the telegraph reshaped how companies operated, how wars were fought, and how news was reported. It was a technological breakthrough that connected the world in ways that had never been possible before, creating a foundation for the modern, interconnected society we live in today.

In the world of business, the telegraph was nothing short of a game-changer. Before its invention, companies relied on letters, messengers, and ships to communicate, which could take days, weeks, or even months depending on the distance. The telegraph eliminated these delays, allowing businesses to send and receive information in real time. This newfound speed transformed industries like trade, finance, and transportation, enabling them to operate more efficiently and expand their reach.

One of the industries most profoundly impacted by the telegraph was the railroad. Railroads were the backbone of industrial economies, moving goods and people across vast distances. However, managing train schedules and preventing accidents was a complex challenge. The telegraph provided a solution by allowing railway operators to communicate instantly with stations and trains along their routes. Dispatchers could coordinate schedules, reroute trains, and respond to emergencies in real time, making rail travel safer and more reliable. This efficiency allowed railroads to expand their networks and play an even greater role in economic growth.

The telegraph also revolutionized financial markets. Stock exchanges, which had previously relied on couriers to deliver price updates, began using the telegraph to transmit financial data almost instantly. Investors could now make decisions based on up-to-date information, and markets became more dynamic and interconnected. For example, the New York Stock Exchange used the telegraph to share stock prices with other cities, creating a national financial network. This ability to exchange information quickly and accurately helped businesses grow and contributed to the rise of global trade.

In addition to transforming business, the telegraph had a profound impact on warfare. Before the telegraph, military leaders often had to rely on messengers or written dispatches to communicate with their troops, which could result in significant delays. The telegraph changed this by allowing commanders to send and receive real-time updates, coordinate troop movements, and manage logistics more effectively. This ability to communicate instantly gave military leaders a strategic advantage, enabling them to respond to changing conditions on the battlefield.

One of the earliest examples of the telegraph's role in warfare was during the Crimean War (1853–1856). British commanders used the telegraph to communicate with officials in London, providing updates on the war effort and receiving instructions from the government. This marked the first time that a war was managed in real time from a distant capital, setting a precedent for modern military strategy.

The American Civil War (1861–1865) further demonstrated the importance of the telegraph in warfare. Both the Union and Confederate armies used telegraph lines to coordinate their operations, gather intelligence, and issue orders. President Abraham Lincoln famously spent hours in the telegraph office, using the technology to stay informed about the progress of the war and communicate directly with his generals. The telegraph allowed the Union to mobilize its resources more effectively, contributing to its eventual victory. It also highlighted the vulnerability of telegraph lines, as both sides frequently targeted them to disrupt enemy communications.

The telegraph's impact extended beyond business and war—it also transformed journalism, ushering in a new era of real-time news reporting. Before the telegraph, news often traveled slowly, arriving days or weeks after an event had occurred. The telegraph changed this by allowing reporters to send updates from the field almost immediately, enabling newspapers to publish breaking news stories. This innovation created a more informed and connected public, as people could now learn about events happening in distant parts of the world in near real time.

The rise of wire services, such as the Associated Press (AP), was a direct result of the telegraph's capabilities. Founded in 1846, the AP used the telegraph to gather and distribute news stories to newspapers across the United States. This allowed smaller publications to access national and international news, leveling the playing field and ensuring that more people had access to important information. The telegraph also enabled newspapers to cover global events, such as wars, political developments, and natural disasters, fostering a sense of global awareness and interconnectedness.

One notable example of the telegraph's impact on journalism was its role in reporting the assassination of President Abraham Lincoln in 1865. News of the assassination was transmitted via telegraph to cities across the United States within hours, allowing newspapers to inform the public almost immediately. This rapid dissemination of information marked a turning point in the history of journalism, demonstrating the power of the telegraph to shape public opinion and create a shared sense of experience.

The telegraph's ability to transmit information quickly and accurately had far-reaching consequences for society. In business, it enabled companies to operate more efficiently, expand their markets, and participate in global trade. In warfare, it gave military leaders a strategic advantage, allowing them to coordinate their forces and respond to changing conditions in real time. In journalism, it created a more informed and connected public, transforming the way people consumed news and understood the world around them.

The Telephone

The invention of the telephone in the late 19th century revolutionized communication, bringing voices across distances and transforming the way people connected with one another. For the first time in history, individuals could speak to each other in real time, no matter how far apart they were. This breakthrough not only improved upon earlier communication technologies, such as the telegraph, but also laid the foundation for the modern, interconnected world we live in today. The telephone became a symbol of progress and modernity, changing personal relationships, business operations, and government communication forever.

The journey to the invention of the telephone was marked by years of experimentation and innovation. While the telegraph had already demonstrated the power of transmitting messages over long distances using electrical signals, it was limited to sending text-based messages in the form of Morse code. The idea of transmitting the human voice electrically was a far more complex challenge. Alexander Graham Bell, a Scottish-born inventor and teacher of the deaf, was one of the pioneers who took on this challenge. Working alongside his assistant, Thomas Watson, Bell developed a device that could convert sound waves into electrical signals and then back into sound waves, allowing voices to be transmitted over a wire.

On March 10, 1876, Bell successfully tested his invention, speaking the now-famous words, "Mr. Watson, come here, I want to see you." Watson, who was in another room, heard Bell's voice clearly through the device, marking the birth of the telephone. Bell's invention was groundbreaking because it allowed for direct, personal, and immediate conversations, something the telegraph could not achieve. While the telegraph required trained operators to encode and decode messages, the telephone enabled anyone to speak and be heard, making communication more natural and accessible.

The telephone quickly gained popularity, and its impact on society was profound. One of the most significant ways the telephone transformed communication was by strengthening personal relationships. Before the telephone, staying in touch with loved ones over long distances often required writing letters, which could take days or weeks to arrive. The telephone changed this by allowing families and friends to hear each other's voices in real time, creating a sense of closeness despite physical separation. A mother could speak to her child studying in another city, or a soldier stationed far from home could hear the comforting voice of a loved one. The telephone brought people together in ways that were previously impossible, making the world feel smaller and more connected.

In addition to transforming personal relationships, the telephone revolutionized business operations. Companies quickly recognized the value of the telephone for coordinating their activities, improving customer service, and expanding their reach. Businesses could now communicate instantly with suppliers, clients, and employees, streamlining operations and increasing efficiency. For example, a factory manager could use the telephone to place an urgent order for raw materials, ensuring that production continued without delays. Retailers could take orders from customers over the phone, providing a level of convenience that had never been possible before. The telephone became an essential ability for commerce, driving economic growth and innovation.

Governments also embraced the telephone as a powerful ability for administration and diplomacy. The ability to communicate instantly allowed government officials to respond more quickly to crises, coordinate policies, and manage their territories more effectively. For example, during emergencies, such as natural disasters or military conflicts, the telephone enabled rapid communication between different branches of government, ensuring a swift and coordinated response. Diplomats used the telephone to negotiate agreements and maintain contact with their counterparts in other countries, making international relations more efficient and dynamic.

The societal impact of the telephone was further amplified by the rapid expansion of telephone networks in the late 19th and early 20th centuries. In the United States, the Bell Telephone Company (founded by Alexander Graham Bell) played a leading role in building the infrastructure needed to connect cities, towns, and rural areas. By the early 20th century, millions of people had access to telephones, and the number of telephone lines continued to grow rapidly. Similar developments occurred in Europe and other parts of the world, as governments and private companies invested in telephone networks to connect their populations.

One of the most remarkable aspects of the telephone's expansion was its ability to bridge social and economic divides. While telephones were initially a luxury item available only to the wealthy, technological advancements and economies of scale eventually made them more affordable and accessible to the general public. By the mid-20th century, telephones had become a common feature in homes and businesses, symbolizing progress and modernity.

The telephone also paved the way for future innovations in communication technology. It laid the groundwork for the development of mobile phones, the internet, and other digital communication systems that continue to shape our world today. The principles behind Bell's invention—converting sound into electrical signals and transmitting them over a network—remain at the heart of modern communication technologies.

Social and Economic Impacts of Early Telecommunications

The invention of early telecommunications technologies, such as the telegraph and telephone, marked a turning point in human history, revolutionizing the way people exchanged information and interacted with one another. These innovations transformed societies and economies by enabling instant communication, something that had been impossible with traditional methods like letters or messengers. The ability to transmit information quickly and reliably over long distances reshaped industries, strengthened personal relationships, and fostered a sense of global interconnectedness that continues to define the modern world.

Before the advent of telecommunications, communication over long distances was slow and unreliable. Messages had to be physically carried by messengers, ships, or postal services, which could take days, weeks, or even months to reach their destination. The telegraph, invented in the early 19th century, changed this by allowing messages to be transmitted almost instantly using electrical signals. Samuel Morse, one of the key pioneers of the telegraph, developed Morse code, a system of dots and dashes that could represent letters and numbers. This innovation made it possible to send detailed messages quickly and accurately over long distances, revolutionizing communication. The telephone, invented by Alexander Graham Bell in 1876, built upon the success of the telegraph by enabling people to transmit their voices in real time. Unlike the telegraph, which required trained operators to encode and decode messages, the telephone allowed for direct, personal conversations, making communication more natural and accessible.

The economic impacts of these technologies were profound. Businesses quickly recognized the value of telecommunications for improving efficiency, expanding markets, and coordinating operations. The telegraph, in particular, became an essential ability for industries like finance, transportation, and trade. In the world of finance, the telegraph revolutionized how stock markets operated. Before the telegraph, stock prices and financial information were transmitted by couriers, which often led to delays and inefficiencies. The telegraph allowed stock exchanges to share real-time data, enabling investors to make faster and more informed decisions. This innovation helped create a more dynamic and interconnected financial system, laying the groundwork for modern global markets.

The transportation industry, especially railroads, also benefited greatly from telecommunications. Railroads were the backbone of industrial economies, moving goods and people across vast distances. However, managing train schedules and preventing accidents was a complex challenge. The telegraph provided a solution by allowing railway operators to communicate instantly with stations and trains along their routes. Dispatchers could coordinate schedules, reroute trains, and respond to emergencies in real time, making rail travel safer and more efficient. This efficiency allowed railroads to expand their networks and play an even greater role in economic growth.

Trade and commerce were similarly transformed by telecommunications. Merchants and traders used the telegraph to negotiate prices, place orders, and coordinate the movement of goods. For example, a merchant in London could use the telegraph to communicate with suppliers in India, ensuring that shipments of tea or spices arrived on time. The telephone further enhanced these capabilities by allowing businesses to have direct conversations, making negotiations faster and more personal. These technologies not only streamlined operations but also enabled businesses to expand their reach, connecting local markets to global trade networks. By connecting distant regions and enabling faster decision-making, the telegraph and telephone contributed to the rise of global commerce, fostering economic growth and creating new opportunities for trade and investment.

The social impacts of early telecommunications were just as transformative as the economic ones. By enabling real-time communication across distances, the telegraph and telephone brought people closer together, reshaping personal relationships and creating new opportunities for social interaction. One of the most significant social impacts of these technologies was their ability to strengthen family ties. Before the telephone, families separated by distance often relied on letters to stay in touch, which could take weeks to arrive. The telephone changed this by allowing people to hear each other's voices in real time, creating a sense of closeness despite physical separation. A parent could speak to a child studying in another city, or a soldier stationed far from home could hear the comforting voice of a loved one. The telephone became a lifeline for maintaining personal connections, making the world feel smaller and more connected.

Telecommunications also played a role in shaping public opinion and spreading information. The telegraph, for example, revolutionized journalism by enabling the rapid transmission of news stories from distant locations. Wire services like the Associated Press used the telegraph to gather and distribute news, allowing newspapers to report on global events in near real time. This innovation created a more informed and connected public, as people could now learn about events happening in other parts of the world almost as they occurred. The telephone further enhanced this capability by allowing journalists to conduct interviews and gather information more quickly and efficiently. The sense of global interconnectedness fostered by telecommunications also had broader social implications. By connecting people and places, these technologies helped break down barriers between cultures and fostered a sense of shared humanity. For example, during times of crisis, such as natural disasters or wars, the telegraph and telephone allowed people to coordinate relief efforts and offer support to those in need. This ability to communicate instantly created new opportunities for collaboration and solidarity, both within and between societies.

The social and economic impacts of early telecommunications technologies, such as the telegraph and telephone, were profound and far-reaching. By enabling instant information exchange, these innovations revolutionized communication, transforming how businesses operated, how people connected with one another, and how societies functioned. The telegraph and telephone not only streamlined economic activities, such as trade, finance, and transportation, but also strengthened personal relationships, shaped public opinion, and fostered a sense of global interconnectedness. These technologies laid the foundation for the modern communication networks that continue to shape our world today, demonstrating the power of innovation to bring people and ideas closer together.

Chapter 7

Radio And Television

The Birth of Radio

The birth of radio was a monumental achievement in the history of communication, transforming the way people shared information and connected with one another. What began as a ability for transmitting Morse code messages across long distances evolved into a powerful medium for broadcasting entertainment, education, and news to mass audiences. The journey from wireless telegraphy to radio broadcasts was marked by groundbreaking scientific discoveries and technological innovations that laid the foundation for modern wireless communication.

The origins of radio can be traced back to the late 19th century, when scientists began exploring the possibility of transmitting messages without the use of wires. One of the key figures in this development was Heinrich Hertz, a German physicist who, in the 1880s, demonstrated the existence of electromagnetic waves. Hertz's experiments proved that these waves could travel through the air, a discovery that would later become the basis for wireless communication. His work inspired other inventors and scientists to explore how electromagnetic waves could be harnessed to transmit information.

Building on Hertz's discoveries, Nikola Tesla and Guglielmo Marconi made significant contributions to the development of radio technology. Tesla, a brilliant inventor, developed early designs for wireless communication systems and demonstrated the ability to transmit signals over short distances. Marconi, often credited as the father of radio, took these ideas further by creating a practical system for long-distance wireless communication. In 1895, Marconi successfully transmitted a wireless signal over a distance of more than a mile, and by 1901, he had achieved the first transatlantic wireless transmission. This breakthrough proved that it was possible to send messages across vast distances without the need for physical connections like telegraph wires.

In its early years, radio was primarily used for point-to-point communication, much like the telegraph. It was particularly valuable in maritime and military contexts, where the ability to send and receive messages over long distances was critical. Ships at sea could use radio to communicate with one another and with shore stations, improving safety and coordination. For example, during the sinking of the Titanic in 1912, the ship's wireless operators sent distress signals that were received by nearby vessels, saving hundreds of lives. In military operations, radio allowed commanders to coordinate troop movements and share intelligence in real time, giving them a strategic advantage.

While early radio was limited to transmitting Morse code messages, the technology soon evolved to include the transmission of voice and music. This transition marked the beginning of radio as a broadcasting medium, capable of reaching large audiences simultaneously. One of the first major milestones in this evolution was achieved by Canadian inventor Reginald Fessenden, who, in 1906, conducted the first successful broadcast of voice and music. On Christmas Eve of that year, Fessenden transmitted a program that included a reading of the Bible and a violin performance, which was heard by operators on ships at sea. This event demonstrated the potential of radio to go beyond point-to-point communication and become a medium for mass communication.

The true birth of radio broadcasting, however, came in the 1920s, when the first commercial radio stations began operating. In 1920, KDKA in Pittsburgh, Pennsylvania, became the first licensed radio station to broadcast regular programs. Its inaugural broadcast covered the results of the U.S. presidential election, marking the beginning of radio as a source of news and information for the public. Other stations soon followed, and radio quickly became a popular medium for entertainment, education, and news dissemination.

The social and cultural impacts of radio's birth were profound. For the first time, people could hear live music, speeches, and news reports from the comfort of their homes. Radio brought entertainment and information to rural areas that had previously been isolated from cultural and political events. Families would gather around their radios to listen to programs, creating a shared experience that brought people closer together. Radio also played a significant role in shaping public opinion, as it allowed leaders and broadcasters to reach large audiences directly. For example, during the 1930s, President Franklin D. Roosevelt used his "fireside chats" to communicate with the American people, offering reassurance and guidance during the Great Depression.

Radio also became a powerful ability for education and cultural exchange. Educational programs brought knowledge to listeners of all ages, while broadcasts of music and drama introduced audiences to new art forms and ideas. Radio helped to break down cultural barriers by exposing people to different perspectives and traditions, fostering a sense of global interconnectedness.

The rise of radio broadcasting also had a significant impact on the entertainment industry. Musicians, actors, and comedians found new opportunities to reach audiences, and radio became a launching pad for many careers. Popular programs, such as variety shows, soap operas, and serialized dramas, captivated listeners and became a central part of daily life. Radio's ability to create vivid mental images through sound alone earned it the nickname "the theater of the mind," as it allowed listeners to imagine the scenes and characters being described.

Radio as a Ability for Propaganda, Entertainment, and Education

Radio emerged as one of the most influential technologies of the 20th century, transforming the way people received information, enjoyed entertainment, and accessed education. Its ability to reach mass audiences in real time made it a powerful medium for shaping public opinion, creating shared cultural experiences, and spreading knowledge. Governments, entertainers, and educators alike recognized the potential of radio to connect with people on an unprecedented scale, and they used it to influence, inspire, and inform.

One of the most significant uses of radio was as a ability for propaganda, particularly during times of war and political upheaval. Governments and political leaders understood that radio could reach millions of people directly, bypassing traditional barriers to communication. In Nazi Germany, Joseph Goebbels, the Minister of

Propaganda, used radio to spread the regime's ideology and control public opinion. The Nazis produced inexpensive radios, known as the "Volksempfänger" (People's Receiver), to ensure that as many Germans as possible could listen to state-approved broadcasts. These programs were carefully crafted to promote Nazi ideals, glorify Adolf Hitler, and demonize the regime's enemies. By saturating the airwaves with propaganda, the Nazis used radio to manipulate public perception and maintain control over the population.

In contrast, Franklin D. Roosevelt in the United States used radio as a ability to reassure and unite the American people during challenging times. His "Fireside Chats," a series of informal radio addresses, were designed to explain government policies and provide comfort during the Great Depression and World War II. Roosevelt's calm and conversational tone made listeners feel as though he was speaking directly to them, fostering a sense of trust and connection. These broadcasts helped to rally public support for New Deal programs and wartime efforts, demonstrating the power of radio to inspire confidence and solidarity.

During World War II, radio played a critical role in rallying support and disseminating information. Allied governments used radio to broadcast messages of hope and resistance to occupied territories, countering enemy propaganda. For example, the BBC's broadcasts to Europe provided news and encouragement to those living under Nazi rule, while programs like "Voice of America" shared the ideals of democracy and freedom. Radio also kept citizens informed about the progress of the war, creating a sense of shared purpose and determination.

Beyond its use as a political ability, radio became a beloved source of entertainment, bringing music, drama, and comedy into people's homes. In the early 20th century, radio revolutionized the entertainment industry by making performances accessible to audiences far beyond the reach of theaters and concert halls. Families would gather around their radios to listen to live music broadcasts, serialized dramas, and variety shows, creating a shared cultural experience that transcended geographic boundaries.

Serialized dramas, often referred to as "radio plays" or "soap operas," became particularly popular. Programs like *The Shadow* and *The Lone Ranger* captivated listeners with their thrilling stories and memorable characters. These shows allowed people to escape from the challenges of daily life and immerse themselves in imaginative worlds. Comedy programs, such as *The Jack Benny Program* and *Amos 'n' Andy*, brought laughter into homes, while live music performances introduced audiences to new genres and artists. Radio also played a key role in popularizing jazz, swing, and other musical styles, shaping the cultural landscape of the time.

The communal nature of radio entertainment created a sense of connection among listeners. People from different backgrounds and regions could tune in to the same programs, fostering a shared cultural identity. Radio stars became household names, and popular catchphrases from shows entered everyday conversation. This ability to bring people together made radio a unifying force in society, bridging divides and creating a sense of belonging.

In addition to its roles in propaganda and entertainment, radio became a powerful ability for education, providing access to information and learning opportunities for people in remote or underserved areas. Educational radio programs were developed to teach literacy, share agricultural advice, and broadcast lectures on a wide range of topics. For example, in the United States, programs like the "National Farm and Home Hour" provided farmers with practical tips and updates on agricultural policies, helping to improve productivity and livelihoods.

In countries with limited access to formal education, radio became a lifeline for learning. Governments and organizations used radio to deliver lessons to children and adults in rural areas, where schools were scarce or nonexistent. These programs covered subjects such as reading, writing, mathematics, and health education, empowering individuals with knowledge and skills. In some cases, radio was even used to teach foreign languages, enabling listeners to connect with the wider world.

Radio also played a role in spreading scientific and cultural knowledge. Programs featuring interviews with experts, discussions on current events, and explorations of history and art brought intellectual enrichment to audiences of all ages. By making education accessible to a broader population, radio contributed to social and intellectual development, helping to close gaps in knowledge and opportunity.

The social and cultural impacts of radio were profound. It became a medium that could entertain, educate, and influence all at once, reaching people in ways that no other technology had before. Radio brought the world into people's homes, connecting them to events, ideas, and cultures beyond their immediate surroundings. It shaped public opinion, created shared experiences, and provided opportunities for learning and growth.

The Golden Age of Television

The Golden Age of Television, spanning the mid-20th century, marked a transformative period in the history of communication and culture. During this time, television emerged as a dominant medium, revolutionizing how people consumed information and entertainment. It became a central part of daily life, shaping cultural norms, influencing public opinion, and creating shared experiences that transcended geographic and social boundaries. With its ability to combine visual storytelling and real-time broadcasting, television redefined how societies connected with the world around them.

The rise of television began in the years following World War II, as technological advancements made it more affordable and accessible to households. By the 1950s, television sets had become a common feature in living rooms across the United States and other parts of the world. Unlike radio, which relied solely on sound, television brought images into people's homes, allowing them to see events, stories, and personalities unfold before their eyes. This visual element made television a uniquely powerful medium, capable of engaging audiences in ways that no other technology could.

Television quickly became a unifying force, creating a shared cultural experience for viewers. Families would gather around their TV sets to watch their favorite programs, from sitcoms and dramas to variety shows and live events. These shared moments brought people together, fostering a sense of connection and community. Television also broke down barriers between different regions and social groups, as people from diverse backgrounds tuned in to the same programs and witnessed the same events. This ability to reach mass audiences made television a defining feature of modern life.

One of the most significant ways television shaped society during its golden age was by influencing public opinion. The medium's ability to broadcast news, political debates, and major events in real time gave it unparalleled power to inform and shape perceptions. A landmark example of this was the televised debates between John F. Kennedy and Richard Nixon during the 1960 U.S. presidential election. These debates were the first in history to be broadcast on television, and they demonstrated the medium's ability to influence political outcomes. Viewers who watched the debates on television were struck by Kennedy's confident and charismatic appearance, while Nixon, who appeared tired and less polished, struggled to make the same impression. The debates highlighted the importance of image and presentation in modern politics, forever changing how campaigns were conducted.

Television also played a crucial role in bringing social issues to the forefront of public consciousness. During the Civil Rights Movement of the 1950s and 1960s, television coverage of protests, marches, and acts of violence against African Americans exposed the harsh realities of racial injustice to a national audience. Images of peaceful demonstrators being attacked by police dogs or sprayed with fire hoses shocked viewers and galvanized support for the movement. By broadcasting these events into millions of homes, television helped to build awareness and empathy, making it a powerful ability for social change.

Beyond its impact on news and politics, television became a cultural force through its entertainment programming. Iconic shows from the golden age of television reflected and influenced societal values and trends, shaping how people thought about family, relationships, and the world around them. Sitcoms like *I Love Lucy* captured the humor and challenges of everyday life, while dramas like *The Twilight*

Zone explored deeper themes of morality and human nature. These programs not only entertained audiences but also provided a mirror to society, offering insights into the hopes, fears, and aspirations of the time.

Variety shows, such as *The Ed Sullivan Show,* introduced viewers to a wide range of talent, from comedians and musicians to dancers and magicians. These programs became cultural touchstones, launching the careers of countless artists and bringing new forms of entertainment into people's homes. One of the most memorable moments in television history occurred in 1964, when The Beatles made their American debut on *The Ed Sullivan Show.* Their performance captivated millions of viewers and marked the beginning of the British Invasion, a cultural phenomenon that reshaped music and popular culture.

Television also brought historic events into people's living rooms, creating moments of collective memory that defined an era. One of the most iconic broadcasts of the golden age was the live coverage of the Apollo 11 moon landing in 1969. An estimated 600 million people around the world watched as Neil Armstrong took his first steps on the lunar surface, uttering the famous words, "That's one small step for man, one giant leap for mankind." This event demonstrated the power of television to unite people across the globe, as viewers shared in the wonder and excitement of a monumental achievement.

In addition to entertainment and news, television served as a platform for education and cultural enrichment. Educational programs, such as *Sesame Street,* which debuted in 1969, used the medium to teach children basic literacy and numeracy skills while promoting social values like kindness and cooperation.

Documentaries and public television programs brought history, science, and the arts to a wider audience, making knowledge more accessible and fostering a love of learning.

The golden age of television was a period of innovation and influence, during which the medium became an integral part of daily life and a powerful ability for shaping culture and public opinion. By bringing visual storytelling into homes, television created shared experiences that transcended boundaries and connected people in new ways. It informed and inspired, entertained and educated, leaving an indelible mark on society. The legacy of this era continues to resonate, as television remains a central part of how we understand and engage with the world around us.

The Role of Broadcast Media in Political and Social Movements

Broadcast media, encompassing radio and television, has been one of the most powerful abilities for shaping and amplifying political and social movements throughout history. By providing platforms for leaders and activists to reach mass audiences, broadcast media has played a pivotal role in spreading messages, rallying support, and inspiring collective action. Its ability to deliver real-time information, evoke emotional responses, and connect people across geographic and cultural divides has made it a transformative force in the fight for justice, equality, and change.

The power of broadcast media to mobilize citizens was evident as early as World War II, when radio became a critical ability for governments and resistance movements alike. Leaders like Winston Churchill used radio to deliver speeches that inspired hope and resilience during the darkest days of the war. Churchill's broadcasts, filled with determination and resolve, united the British people and strengthened their resolve to endure. At the same time, radio was used by resistance groups in occupied Europe to coordinate efforts against Nazi forces, spreading messages of defiance and solidarity. The immediacy of radio allowed these messages to reach people quickly, even in the most remote or oppressed areas, making it an indispensable ability for mobilization.

In the decades that followed, television emerged as a dominant medium, bringing political and social struggles into the homes of millions. One of the most powerful examples of this was the role of television during the Civil Rights Movement in the United States. Leaders like Martin Luther King Jr. understood the importance of broadcast media in exposing the realities of racial injustice and rallying support for the cause. King's speeches, such as his iconic "I Have a Dream" address during the 1963 March on Washington, were broadcast to audiences across the nation, inspiring hope and determination. More importantly, television coverage of events like the Selma to Montgomery marches and the brutal treatment of peaceful protesters in Birmingham, Alabama, shocked viewers and galvanized public opinion. Images of police using fire hoses and attack dogs against unarmed demonstrators revealed the harsh realities of segregation and discrimination, forcing the nation to confront its moral failings.

Broadcast media has also been a powerful ability for exposing injustices and challenging authority. During the Vietnam War, television played a crucial role in shaping public opinion and fueling anti-war protests. For the first time, Americans could see the realities of war unfold on their screens. Graphic footage of combat, civilian casualties, and the suffering of soldiers brought the horrors of the conflict into living rooms across the country. This unfiltered coverage sparked widespread outrage and led to a growing anti-war movement, as people demanded an end to the violence. The immediacy and emotional impact of television made it impossible to ignore the human cost of the war, ultimately influencing government policy and accelerating the withdrawal of U.S. forces.

Radio, too, has been a vital ability for social and political movements, particularly in regions where access to other forms of media was limited. In Africa and Asia, radio played a key role in anti-colonial movements, helping to unite people in their struggles for independence. Leaders and activists used radio to spread messages of resistance, educate the public about their rights, and inspire collective action. For example, during the Algerian War of Independence, the National Liberation Front (FLN) used clandestine radio broadcasts to communicate with supporters and counter French propaganda. Similarly, in India, radio was used to mobilize support for the independence movement, spreading the messages of leaders like Mahatma Gandhi to rural and urban audiences alike.

The emotional power of broadcast media lies in its ability to connect people to events and stories in a deeply personal way. Unlike print media, which relies on words alone, radio and television combine sound, imagery, and emotion to create a more immersive experience. This immediacy allows audiences to feel as though they are witnessing history as it happens, fostering empathy and a sense of shared purpose. For example, during the fall of the Berlin Wall in 1989, live television coverage captured the joy and hope of East and West Germans as they reunited after decades of division. These broadcasts not only documented a historic moment but also inspired movements for freedom and democracy around the world.

Broadcast media has also been instrumental in amplifying the voices of marginalized communities and giving them a platform to share their stories. In the 1960s and 1970s, feminist and LGBTQ+ movements used radio and television to challenge societal norms and advocate for equality. Programs and interviews featuring activists brought their struggles and demands to a wider audience, helping to build awareness and support. Similarly, Indigenous communities have used radio to preserve their languages and cultures, ensuring that their voices are heard in a rapidly changing world.

Chapter 8

The Internet Revolution

inventions in human history, can be traced back to the late 1960s with the creation of ARPANET. What began as a secure communication network for researchers and military organizations evolved into a global platform that connects billions of people today. The journey from ARPANET to the World Wide Web is a story of innovation, collaboration, and technological breakthroughs that forever changed how we communicate, share information, and interact with the world.

ARPANET, the precursor to the modern internet, was developed by the U.S. Department of Defense's Advanced Research Projects Agency (ARPA). During the Cold War, there was a pressing need for a communication system that could withstand potential disruptions, such as a nuclear attack. Traditional communication networks relied on centralized systems, which were vulnerable to failure if a single point was damaged. ARPA sought to create a decentralized network that could continue functioning even if parts of it were destroyed. This vision led to the development of ARPANET, which became operational in 1969.

The key technological breakthrough that made ARPANET possible was packet switching. Unlike traditional communication methods, which relied on dedicated circuits to transmit data, packet switching broke information into smaller packets. These packets could travel independently across the network and be reassembled at their destination. This method was not only more efficient but also more resilient, as packets could take alternate routes if one part of the network was compromised. The concept of packet switching was pioneered by researchers like Paul Baran and Donald Davies, and it became the foundation of modern networking.

Another critical development was the creation of protocols that allowed computers to communicate with one another. In the early 1970s, researchers Vinton Cerf and Robert Kahn developed the Transmission Control Protocol/Internet Protocol (TCP/IP). These protocols standardized how data was transmitted and received across networks, enabling different types of computers to connect and share information seamlessly. TCP/IP became the backbone of ARPANET and, later, the internet.

Initially, ARPANET was used to connect a small number of research institutions and military organizations. The first message sent over ARPANET occurred on October 29, 1969, between a computer at UCLA and one at Stanford Research Institute. The message was meant to be the word "LOGIN," but the system crashed after the first two letters, sending only "LO." Despite this humble beginning, ARPANET quickly expanded, linking more universities and research centers. By the 1970s, it had become a vital ability for academic collaboration, allowing researchers to share data, access remote computers, and communicate via email, which was introduced in 1971.

As ARPANET grew, it began to connect with other networks, creating the foundation for a global system. By the 1980s, the term "internet" was being used to describe this interconnected network of networks. The adoption of TCP/IP as the standard protocol in 1983 further unified these networks, making it easier for them to communicate with one another. The internet was no longer just a military or academic ability; it was becoming a platform with the potential to connect the world.

The next major leap in the internet's evolution came in 1989, when Tim Berners-Lee, a British computer scientist working at CERN, proposed the creation of the World Wide Web. While the internet provided the infrastructure for connecting computers, the World Wide Web made it accessible and user-friendly for the general public. Berners-Lee introduced three key innovations that transformed the internet: hypertext, web browsers, and URLs (Uniform Resource Locators).

Hypertext allowed users to click on links and navigate between different documents and resources, creating a seamless and intuitive way to access information. Web browsers, such as the first one developed by Berners-Lee called WorldWideWeb (later renamed Nexus), provided a graphical interface for users to interact with the web. URLs standardized how web addresses were identified, making it easy to locate and access specific resources. Together, these innovations turned the internet into a platform for communication, commerce, and information sharing on a global scale.

The World Wide Web was officially launched in 1991, and its impact was immediate. For the first time, people could access information from anywhere in the world with just a few clicks. The web democratized knowledge, breaking down barriers to education and information. It also created new opportunities for businesses, enabling e-commerce and digital marketing. Websites became virtual storefronts, and companies could reach customers in ways that were previously unimaginable.

The social and cultural impact of the World Wide Web was equally profound. It revolutionized how people communicated, allowing them to send emails, participate in online forums, and connect through social media platforms that would emerge in the following decades. The web also became a platform for creativity and self-expression, giving individuals the ability to share their ideas, art, and stories with a global audience.

How the Internet Transformed Communication, Business, and Society

The internet has transformed the world in ways that were unimaginable just a few decades ago. It has revolutionized how people communicate, reshaped the way businesses operate, and fundamentally altered the fabric of society. By enabling instant global connectivity, creating new economic opportunities, and fostering cultural exchange, the internet has become an integral part of daily life, shaping how we learn, work, and interact with one another.

One of the most profound impacts of the internet has been on communication. Before its advent, long-distance communication was often slow and expensive, relying on letters, phone calls, or fax machines. The internet changed this by enabling instant global connectivity. Email, one of the earliest and most widely used internet applications, allowed people to send messages across the world in seconds, revolutionizing personal and professional communication. Messaging apps like WhatsApp, Telegram, and

Facebook Messenger further enhanced this ability by enabling real-time text, voice, and video communication, making it easier than ever to stay connected with friends, family, and colleagues, no matter where they are.

The rise of social media platforms has taken internet-based communication to an entirely new level. Platforms like Facebook, Twitter, Instagram, and TikTok have allowed individuals to share ideas, build communities, and engage in real-time interactions on a global scale. Social media has given people a voice, enabling them to express themselves, connect with like-minded individuals, and participate in conversations that transcend geographic and cultural boundaries. It has also become a powerful ability for activism, allowing social movements to gain momentum and reach wider audiences. For example, movements like #BlackLivesMatter and #MeToo have used social media to raise awareness, mobilize supporters, and drive social change.

In addition to transforming communication, the internet has reshaped the world of business. It has created new opportunities for e-commerce, digital marketing, and remote work, fundamentally changing how companies operate and interact with their customers. Online retail giants like Amazon and eBay have revolutionized shopping by allowing consumers to purchase products from the comfort of their homes and have them delivered to their doorsteps. These platforms have also provided small businesses and entrepreneurs with access to global markets, enabling them to reach customers far beyond their local communities.

The internet has also transformed how businesses market their products and services. Digital marketing, which includes strategies like search engine optimization (SEO), social media advertising, and email campaigns, has allowed companies to target specific audiences with precision and measure the effectiveness of their efforts in real time. Platforms like Google Ads and Facebook Ads have made it possible for businesses of all sizes to compete on a level playing field, reaching potential customers wherever they are online.

Another significant impact of the internet on business has been the rise of remote work and cloud computing. The internet has made it possible for employees to work from anywhere, using abilities like Zoom, Microsoft Teams, and Slack to collaborate with colleagues in real time. Cloud computing services like Google Drive, Dropbox, and Amazon Web Services (AWS) have enabled businesses to store and access data securely from any location, streamlining operations and reducing costs. Digital payment systems like PayPal, Stripe, and mobile payment apps have further facilitated online transactions, making it easier for businesses and consumers to exchange money in a fast and secure manner.

The societal impacts of the internet are equally profound. One of its most significant contributions has been the democratization of access to information. Before the internet, knowledge was often confined to libraries, universities, and other institutions, making it difficult for many people to access. The internet has changed this by making vast amounts of information available to anyone with an internet connection. Search engines like Google and online encyclopedias like Wikipedia have made it possible for people to learn about virtually any topic with just a few clicks. Online courses and educational platforms like Coursera, Khan Academy, and Duolingo have further expanded access to learning, empowering individuals to acquire new skills and knowledge at their own pace.

The internet has also fostered cultural exchange, allowing people from different parts of the world to share their traditions, art, and ideas. Social media platforms, video-sharing sites like YouTube, and streaming services like Netflix have exposed audiences to diverse perspectives and experiences, breaking down cultural barriers and promoting understanding. At the same time, the internet has empowered marginalized communities by giving them a platform to share their stories and advocate for their rights.

However, the internet's transformative power has not come without challenges. Digital inequality remains a significant issue, as millions of people around the world still lack access to reliable internet connections. This digital divide has created disparities in education, economic opportunities, and access to information, particularly in developing countries. The internet has also given rise to new problems, such as the spread of misinformation and the erosion of privacy. Social media platforms have been criticized for enabling the rapid dissemination of false information, which can influence public opinion and undermine trust in institutions. Additionally, the collection and use of personal data by companies and governments have raised concerns about surveillance and the loss of individual privacy.

Despite these challenges, the internet's impact on communication, business, and society has been overwhelmingly transformative. It has connected people across the globe, created new economic opportunities, and empowered individuals to learn, share, and innovate. The internet has become a cornerstone of modern life, shaping how we interact with one another and the world around us. As we continue to navigate its complexities, the internet's potential to drive progress and bring people together remains one of its most remarkable achievements.

The Rise of Social Media

The rise of social media has transformed the way people connect, communicate, and share information, creating a new digital landscape that has reshaped modern life. Platforms like Facebook, Twitter, Instagram, and TikTok have revolutionized communication by enabling instant, global interactions. They have allowed individuals to share their voices, build communities, and engage with others on an unprecedented scale. However, while social media has brought people closer together and empowered social movements, it has also introduced significant challenges, including societal divisions, the spread of misinformation, and ethical concerns.

Social media began as a way for people to connect with friends and family online, but it quickly evolved into something much larger. Facebook, launched in 2004, became one of the first platforms to bring social networking to the mainstream, allowing users to create profiles, share updates, and interact with others. Twitter, introduced in 2006, revolutionized communication by limiting posts to 140 characters (later expanded to 280), encouraging concise and real-time updates. Instagram, launched in 2010, focused on visual storytelling through photos and videos, while TikTok, which gained global popularity in the late 2010s, introduced short-form video content that encouraged creativity and entertainment. These platforms, along with others, have created a digital ecosystem where billions of people interact daily.

One of the most significant impacts of social media has been its ability to foster connections and build communities. Social media has allowed people to stay in touch with loved ones, reconnect with old friends, and meet new people who share similar interests. It has also provided a platform for individuals to share their ideas, talents, and stories with a global audience. For example, artists, writers, and musicians can showcase their work to millions of people, while small businesses can reach customers far beyond their local communities. Social media has broken down geographic barriers, making the world feel smaller and more interconnected.

Beyond personal connections, social media has played a powerful role in empowering social and political movements. It has given marginalized voices a platform to be heard and has amplified calls for justice and equality. One of the most notable examples is the Arab Spring, a series of pro-democracy uprisings that began in 2010. Social media platforms like Facebook and Twitter were used to organize protests, share information, and document events in real time, helping to mobilize millions of people across the Middle East and North Africa. Similarly, the #MeToo movement, which gained momentum in 2017, used social media to raise awareness about sexual harassment and assault, encouraging survivors to share their stories and hold perpetrators accountable. The Black Lives Matter movement has also relied heavily on social media to highlight racial injustices, organize protests, and demand systemic change. These examples demonstrate how social media can be a catalyst for social and political change, empowering individuals to take collective action and challenge the status quo.

However, the rise of social media has not been without its challenges. While it has brought people together, it has also contributed to societal divisions. One of the most significant issues is the creation of echo chambers, where users are exposed primarily to content that aligns with their existing beliefs. Social media algorithms, designed to maximize engagement, often prioritize content that generates strong emotional reactions, such as outrage or fear. This can lead to the amplification of divisive content and the spread of misinformation, further polarizing societies. For example, during elections, false or misleading information can spread rapidly on social media, influencing public opinion and undermining trust in democratic institutions.

The spread of misinformation is a particularly pressing concern. Social media platforms have been criticized for allowing fake news and conspiracy theories to thrive, often with real-world consequences. For instance, during the COVID-19 pandemic, false information about the virus, vaccines, and treatments circulated widely on social media, complicating efforts to combat the crisis. The rapid dissemination of misinformation highlights the need for greater accountability and regulation in the digital space.

Social media has also raised ethical and regulatory challenges, particularly around privacy and online harassment. Many platforms collect vast amounts of personal data from their users, raising concerns about how this information is used and who has access to it. High-profile data breaches and scandals, such as the Cambridge Analytica incident, have underscored the risks associated with the misuse of personal information. Additionally, social media has become a breeding ground for online harassment, bullying, and hate speech, creating a toxic environment for many users. These issues have prompted calls for stricter regulations and greater transparency from social media companies.

Despite these challenges, social media remains a powerful ability for connection and change. It has democratized access to information, giving people the ability to share their stories and engage with others on a global scale. It has also fostered cultural exchange, allowing people from different backgrounds to learn from one another and celebrate their diversity. At its best, social media has the potential to unite people, inspire creativity, and drive progress.

Challenges of the Digital Age

The digital age has brought about incredible advancements, transforming the way we live, work, and connect with one another. However, alongside these benefits, it has also introduced significant challenges that affect individuals, businesses, and governments alike. Among the most pressing issues of the digital age are concerns about privacy, the spread of misinformation, and the growing importance of cybersecurity. These challenges highlight the complexities of navigating a world increasingly shaped by digital technologies and the internet.

One of the most significant challenges of the digital age is the issue of privacy. The rise of digital technologies has revolutionized how personal data is collected, stored, and used. Every time we browse the internet, use social media, or shop online, we leave behind a trail of data—our search history, location, preferences, and even personal details like our names and addresses. This data is often collected by companies to improve their services, target advertisements, or sell to third parties. While this can make our online experiences more convenient, it also raises serious concerns about how our personal information is being used and who has access to it.

Data breaches are one of the most visible threats to privacy in the digital age. When companies or organizations fail to protect the data they collect, it can fall into the hands of hackers or malicious actors.

High-profile breaches, such as the 2017 Equifax breach that exposed the personal information of over 140 million people, demonstrate the risks of storing sensitive data online. These breaches can lead to identity theft, financial loss, and a loss of trust in digital systems.

Surveillance is another major concern. Governments and corporations have the ability to monitor online activity on an unprecedented scale. While surveillance can be used to enhance security and prevent crime, it also raises questions about the balance between safety and individual freedoms. For example, whistleblower Edward Snowden revealed in 2013 that the U.S. National Security Agency (NSA) was conducting mass surveillance programs, collecting data on millions of people without their knowledge. These revelations sparked a global debate about privacy and the ethical limits of surveillance in the digital age.

The misuse of personal information by corporations is yet another issue. Social media platforms, for instance, collect vast amounts of data about their users, which can be used to influence behavior. The Cambridge Analytica scandal in 2018 revealed how data from millions of Facebook users was harvested without their consent and used to target political advertisements during elections. This incident highlighted the need for greater transparency and accountability in how companies handle personal data.

In addition to privacy concerns, the digital age has also given rise to the challenge of misinformation. The internet and social media have made it easier than ever to share information, but they have also enabled the rapid spread of false or misleading content. Misinformation can take many forms, from fake news articles and doctored images to conspiracy theories and propaganda. The speed and reach of the internet mean that misinformation can spread quickly, often outpacing efforts to correct it.

The impact of misinformation on society is profound. It can shape public opinion, influence elections, and erode trust in institutions. For example, during the 2016 U.S. presidential election, fake news stories circulated widely on social media, with some studies suggesting that they may have influenced voter behavior. Similarly, during the COVID-19 pandemic, misinformation about the virus, vaccines, and treatments spread rapidly online, complicating efforts to combat the crisis and putting lives at risk.

One of the reasons misinformation is so difficult to combat is the role of algorithms in shaping what people see online. Social media platforms use algorithms to prioritize content that is likely to engage users, often favoring sensational or emotionally charged posts. This can create echo chambers, where users are exposed only to information that reinforces their existing beliefs, making it harder to distinguish fact from fiction. The challenge of combating misinformation requires a combination of media literacy, fact-checking, and greater accountability from tech companies.

The third major challenge of the digital age is cybersecurity. As more of our lives move online, the need to protect digital systems from threats has become increasingly important. Cyberattacks, such as hacking, ransomware, and phishing, have become more frequent and sophisticated, posing risks to individuals, businesses, and governments.

Hacking involves gaining unauthorized access to computer systems, often to steal sensitive information or disrupt operations. For example, in 2020, the SolarWinds cyberattack targeted multiple

U.S. government agencies and private companies, compromising sensitive data and highlighting the vulnerability of even the most secure systems. Ransomware attacks, where hackers encrypt a victim's data and demand payment to restore access, have also become a growing threat. These attacks can disrupt critical infrastructure, such as hospitals and energy grids, with devastating consequences.

Phishing, another common cyber threat, involves tricking individuals into revealing sensitive information, such as passwords or credit card numbers, by posing as a trustworthy entity. These attacks often come in the form of fake emails or websites and can lead to financial loss and identity theft.

The consequences of cyberattacks extend beyond financial damage. They can undermine trust in digital systems, disrupt economies, and even pose risks to national security. As the digital age continues to evolve, the need for stronger cybersecurity measures has become more urgent. This includes investing in advanced technologies to detect and prevent cyber threats, educating individuals about online safety, and fostering international cooperation to address cybercrime.

Chapter 9

Information As A Ability For Power And Control

Throughout history, rulers, empires, and religious leaders have understood the immense power of controlling information. By shaping what people know, believe, and share, they were able to maintain authority, influence societies, and shape public opinion. From ancient kings to powerful empires and religious institutions, the control of information has been a key strategy for consolidating power and ensuring stability. This practice, while often subtle, has left a profound mark on the development of civilizations and the way societies function.

In the ancient world, kings and emperors used information control to legitimize their rule and project their power. In Mesopotamia, one of the earliest civilizations, rulers like Hammurabi of Babylon used inscriptions to communicate their authority and laws. The famous Code of Hammurabi, carved into a large stone stele, was not just a legal document but also a ability of propaganda. By inscribing the laws in stone and placing the stele in a public space, Hammurabi reinforced his image as a just and divinely chosen ruler. The inscription also ensured that his authority extended across his kingdom, as the laws were presented as unchangeable and sacred.

In ancient Egypt, the pharaohs controlled information through monumental architecture and inscriptions. Temples, statues, and obelisks were adorned with hieroglyphs that celebrated the pharaoh's divine status and military victories. These messages were carefully crafted to present the ruler as a god-king, chosen by the gods to maintain order and prosperity. By controlling the narrative of their reign, pharaohs ensured loyalty and obedience from their subjects. For example, the Great Pyramid of Giza was not just a tomb but also a symbol of the pharaoh's power and connection to the divine, visible to all who lived in its shadow.

Similarly, in ancient China, emperors used information control to reinforce their authority. The "Mandate of Heaven" was a concept that justified the emperor's rule as divinely ordained. To maintain this mandate, Chinese emperors commissioned official records and histories that portrayed their reigns in a favorable light. The control of written records ensured that future generations would view the emperor's rule as legitimate and just. Additionally, the Chinese imperial court controlled the dissemination of knowledge by regulating access to important texts and limiting the spread of ideas that could challenge the emperor's authority.

As civilizations grew into vast empires, the need to control information became even more critical. The Roman Empire, for example, relied on a sophisticated system of information management to maintain order across its vast territories. Public announcements, known as *edicta*, were used to communicate imperial decrees, laws, and policies to the population. These announcements were often inscribed on stone tablets or displayed in public spaces, ensuring that the emperor's authority was visible and respected throughout the empire.

The Romans also used censuses to gather information about their subjects, including population numbers, property ownership, and tax obligations. This information allowed the empire to maintain control over its resources and enforce its policies effectively. At the same time, Roman emperors used propaganda to shape public opinion. Coins, for instance, were minted with images and inscriptions that celebrated the emperor's achievements and virtues, subtly reinforcing loyalty and unity among the people.

Religious leaders and institutions have also played a significant role in controlling information to preserve their influence. During the Middle Ages, the Catholic Church held immense power over European society, in part because it controlled access to sacred texts and knowledge. The Bible, written in Latin, was inaccessible to most people, as only clergy and scholars were educated in the language. This allowed the Church to interpret and teach the Bible's messages as it saw fit, ensuring that its authority remained unchallenged.

The Church also suppressed ideas and writings that it deemed heretical or dangerous. For example, during the Inquisition, individuals who questioned Church doctrine or promoted alternative beliefs were often persecuted. Books and writings that contradicted the Church's teachings were banned or destroyed. This control over knowledge ensured that the Church remained the central authority in both spiritual and political matters.

One of the most significant challenges to the Church's control of information came during the Reformation in the 16th century. The invention of the printing press allowed for the mass production of books, including translations of the Bible into vernacular languages. Figures like Martin Luther used this technology to spread their ideas and challenge the Church's authority. The Reformation demonstrated how the control of information could be both a source of power and a vulnerability, as the spread of new ideas ultimately weakened the Church's dominance.

The control of information by kings, empires, and religious leaders was not always about suppression; it was also about creating a shared identity and sense of order. By shaping the narratives of their rule, these leaders were able to unify their societies and maintain stability. However, this control often came at the cost of freedom and diversity of thought, as alternative perspectives were silenced or marginalized.

Propaganda and Censorship in the Modern Era

Propaganda and censorship have been powerful abilities in the modern era, used by governments, organizations, and individuals to shape public opinion, control information, and maintain power. From the world wars of the 20th century to the digital age of the 21st century, these practices have evolved alongside technology, becoming more sophisticated and far-reaching. While propaganda seeks to influence and persuade, often by manipulating emotions and presenting biased or misleading information, censorship works to suppress dissent, limit access to information, and control narratives. Together, they have played a central role in shaping societies and political landscapes across the globe.

The rise of propaganda as a systematic ability can be traced back to major historical events like World War I and World War II. During World War I, governments recognized the importance of controlling public sentiment to maintain support for the war effort. Propaganda was used to rally citizens, encourage enlistment, and demonize the enemy. Posters with slogans like "Your Country Needs You" and images of heroic soldiers or villainous enemies were plastered across cities, appealing to patriotism and fear. Propaganda films and speeches further reinforced these messages, creating a unified narrative that kept the public engaged and supportive.

World War II saw an even more extensive use of propaganda, with both the Axis and Allied powers employing it to achieve their goals. In Nazi Germany, propaganda became a cornerstone of Adolf Hitler's regime. Under the direction of Joseph Goebbels, the Minister of Propaganda, the Nazi government used films, radio broadcasts, newspapers, and posters to spread its ideology. Messages glorifying Hitler, promoting Aryan supremacy, and vilifying Jews and other minority groups were disseminated to manipulate public opinion and justify the regime's actions. The Nazis also used propaganda to maintain morale during the war, portraying Germany as a strong and righteous nation destined for victory.

On the Allied side, propaganda was used to boost morale, promote unity, and encourage support for the war effort. In the United States, posters like "Rosie the Riveter" encouraged women to join the workforce, while films and newsreels highlighted the bravery of soldiers and the importance of defeating fascism. The British government used radio broadcasts, such as those by Winston Churchill, to inspire resilience and determination among its citizens. Propaganda during World War II was not just about winning battles on the front lines but also about winning hearts and minds at home.

Censorship often went hand in hand with propaganda, as governments sought to control the flow of information and suppress dissenting voices. Authoritarian regimes, in particular, have relied heavily on censorship to maintain power. In the Soviet Union, the government controlled all media, ensuring that only state-approved narratives were published. Independent journalism was nonexistent, and any criticism of the government was harshly punished. The Soviet regime also rewrote history, erasing individuals who fell out of favor from official records and photographs, a practice known as "historical revisionism."

In modern China, censorship has taken on a new form with the advent of the internet. The "Great Firewall of China" is a sophisticated system that blocks access to foreign websites, censors online content, and monitors internet activity. Social media platforms in China are heavily regulated, with posts that criticize the government or discuss sensitive topics quickly removed. This level of control allows the Chinese government to shape public discourse and prevent the spread of ideas that could challenge its authority.

Even democratic governments have employed censorship during times of crisis, particularly during wartime. For example, during World War II, the U.S. government restricted media coverage of certain events to maintain morale and prevent sensitive information from reaching the enemy. While such measures are often justified as necessary for national security, they raise important questions about the balance between freedom of speech and the need for control in extraordinary circumstances.

In the digital age, propaganda and censorship have evolved in ways that were unimaginable in the past. The internet and social media have created new opportunities for spreading information, but they have also made it easier to manipulate and control narratives. State-sponsored disinformation campaigns, for example, have become a common tactic in modern geopolitics. Governments and organizations use fake accounts, bots, and algorithmic manipulation to spread propaganda and influence public opinion. These campaigns often target elections, social movements, and international relations, creating confusion and division.

One of the most concerning aspects of modern propaganda is its ability to exploit algorithms on social media platforms. Algorithms are designed to prioritize content that generates engagement, such as likes, shares, and comments. This often means that sensational, emotionally charged, or polarizing content is amplified, regardless of its accuracy. As a result, propaganda and misinformation can spread rapidly, reaching millions of people before fact-checkers or authorities can intervene. This has had a profound impact on democracy, as false information can sway public opinion, undermine trust in institutions, and influence election outcomes.

Censorship in the digital age has also become more complex. While traditional forms of censorship involved controlling newspapers, radio, and television, modern censorship often involves controlling online platforms. Governments can block websites, shut down internet access, or pressure tech companies to remove content. For example, during political protests or uprisings, some governments have resorted to internet blackouts to prevent activists from organizing or sharing information. At the same time, tech companies themselves have become gatekeepers of information, deciding what content is allowed on their platforms. This raises ethical questions about the role of private corporations in regulating speech and the potential for abuse of power.

The challenges posed by propaganda and censorship in the modern era are significant. They threaten the principles of democracy, freedom of speech, and public trust. Combating these issues requires a multifaceted approach, including media literacy education, greater transparency from tech companies, and international cooperation to address disinformation campaigns. It also requires individuals to critically evaluate the information they consume and share, recognizing the potential for manipulation in the digital age.

The Role of Corporations in Shaping Public Opinion

"In a world of advertising, the customer is not just buying a product; they are buying into a story." – Seth Godin

Corporations have long played a significant role in shaping public opinion, using their resources and influence to craft narratives, promote their interests, and align societal values with their goals. From the rise of mass advertising in the 20th century to the targeted campaigns of the digital age, corporations have become powerful architects of public perception. Through advertising, media ownership, and strategic communication, they have influenced how people think, what they buy, and even how they view critical social, political, and environmental issues.

The rise of corporate influence began in the early 20th century, as companies recognized the power of advertising to shape consumer behavior. With the advent of mass media, such as newspapers, radio, and later television, corporations gained access to large audiences, allowing them to promote their products and services on an unprecedented scale. Advertising campaigns were not just about selling goods—they were about creating desires, shaping lifestyles, and building brand loyalty. For example, Coca-Cola's iconic advertisements in the mid-20th century didn't just sell a beverage; they sold an image of happiness, togetherness, and celebration. Similarly, automobile companies like Ford and General Motors used advertising to associate their cars with freedom, status, and modernity, influencing how people viewed transportation and mobility.

Corporations also leveraged mass media to craft narratives that aligned with their values and interests. By sponsoring television programs, radio shows, and print publications, companies ensured that their messages reached audiences in subtle yet effective ways. For instance, during the 1950s and 1960s, tobacco companies heavily advertised cigarettes as symbols of sophistication and independence, despite growing evidence of their health risks. These campaigns shaped public perception of smoking for decades, demonstrating how corporations could use media to influence societal attitudes.

As the digital age emerged, corporations extended their influence even further, using new technologies and platforms to shape public discourse. Social media platforms like Facebook, Instagram, and Twitter became powerful abilities for corporations to engage directly with consumers, build communities around their brands, and promote their values. Targeted advertising, enabled by algorithms and data analytics, allowed companies to deliver personalized messages to specific audiences, making their campaigns more effective than ever before. For example, companies like Nike have used social media to align their brands with social and political causes, such as racial equality and gender empowerment, appealing to younger, socially conscious consumers.

Public relations (PR) campaigns have also become a key strategy for corporations to shape public opinion on broader issues. Many companies have launched campaigns promoting sustainability, diversity, and corporate social responsibility, positioning themselves as leaders in addressing global challenges. For instance, tech companies like Apple and Google have emphasized their commitment to renewable energy and reducing carbon emissions, using these initiatives to enhance their reputations and build trust with consumers. Similarly, fast-food chains like McDonald's have introduced campaigns highlighting healthier menu options and sustainable sourcing practices, responding to growing public concerns about health and the environment.

However, corporate influence is not limited to consumer behavior— it also extends to social, political, and environmental issues. Corporations often use their power to sway public opinion and influence legislation through lobbying efforts, partnerships with think tanks, and funding for research. For example, oil and gas companies have historically funded campaigns that downplay the risks of climate change, shaping public debates and delaying regulatory action. On the other hand, some corporations have used their influence to advocate for positive change, such as supporting LGBTQ+ rights or promoting education initiatives in underserved communities.

The ethical implications of corporate influence are complex and multifaceted. On one hand, corporations have the resources and reach to drive positive change, raise awareness about important issues, and contribute to societal progress. For example, campaigns promoting sustainability or diversity can inspire individuals and other organizations to take action, creating a ripple effect of positive impact. On the other hand, the concentration of corporate power raises concerns about manipulation, misinformation, and the erosion of democratic values.

One major concern is the spread of misinformation. In their efforts to protect their interests, some corporations have been accused of misleading the public or obscuring the truth. For instance, during the 20th century, the tobacco industry funded research that downplayed the health risks of smoking, delaying public awareness and regulatory action. Similarly, in the digital age, tech giants like Facebook and Google have faced criticism for allowing the spread of fake news and disinformation on their platforms, raising questions about their responsibility in moderating content and protecting public trust.

Another concern is the concentration of media ownership. As corporations acquire media outlets, they gain greater control over the narratives presented to the public. This can lead to biased reporting, limited diversity of perspectives, and the prioritization of corporate interests over journalistic integrity. For example, media conglomerates like Rupert Murdoch's News Corp have been criticized for using their platforms to promote specific political agendas, influencing public opinion on a wide range of issues.

The role of corporate-funded think tanks and research organizations also raises ethical questions. While these institutions often produce valuable insights, their funding sources can influence the conclusions they reach and the policies they advocate. For example, think tanks funded by fossil fuel companies have been accused of downplaying the urgency of climate change, shaping public debates in ways that align with corporate interests.

Despite these challenges, it is important to recognize that corporate influence is not inherently negative. When wielded responsibly, it can drive innovation, raise awareness, and contribute to societal progress. For example, campaigns promoting renewable energy, gender equality, and mental health awareness have had a positive impact, inspiring individuals and organizations to take action. The key lies in ensuring transparency, accountability, and ethical practices in how corporations use their influence.

Information Networks as Abilities of Resistance and Revolution

Throughout history, information networks have been powerful abilities for resistance and revolution, enabling individuals and groups to challenge authority, organize movements, and inspire change. Whether through underground printing presses, secret correspondence, or modern digital platforms, these networks have allowed people to share ideas, coordinate actions, and mobilize support in the face of oppression. They have played a central role in some of the most significant revolutions and resistance movements, demonstrating the transformative power of communication in the fight for freedom and justice.

In the past, information networks relied on physical methods of communication to spread revolutionary ideas and organize resistance. During the American Revolution, for example, secret correspondence and underground printing presses were essential abilities for the colonists. Pamphlets like Thomas Paine's *Common Sense* circulated widely, inspiring people to question British rule and rallying support for independence. These printed materials were often distributed in secret, bypassing British censors and reaching a broad audience. Similarly, committees of correspondence were established to share information between colonies, ensuring that revolutionaries could coordinate their efforts and stay informed about British actions.

The French Revolution also relied heavily on information networks to spread revolutionary ideas and mobilize the population. Revolutionary leaders used pamphlets, newspapers, and public speeches to challenge the monarchy and promote the ideals of liberty, equality, and fraternity. These materials were often produced and distributed by underground networks, bypassing the control of the monarchy and reaching people across France. The ability to share information quickly and effectively helped to unite the revolutionaries and build momentum for change.

Anti-colonial movements in the 19th and 20th centuries also made use of information networks to resist imperial rule. In India, for example, leaders like Mahatma Gandhi used newspapers and pamphlets to spread the message of nonviolent resistance and mobilize support for independence from British rule. These materials were often printed in local languages, ensuring that they could reach a wide audience and inspire collective action. Similarly, in Africa and Southeast Asia, underground networks of activists used secret correspondence and coded messages to organize resistance against colonial powers, demonstrating the enduring power of information in the fight for freedom.

In the modern era, digital information networks have become even more powerful abilities for resistance and revolution. The rise of the internet, social media platforms, and encrypted messaging apps has transformed how people communicate and organize, enabling movements to reach global audiences and operate in real time. One of the most notable examples of this is the Arab Spring, a series of pro-democracy uprisings that swept across the Middle East and North Africa in the early 2010s. Social media platforms like Facebook and Twitter played a central role in these movements, allowing activists to share information, organize protests, and document government abuses.

In Tunisia, for example, the self-immolation of Mohamed Bouazizi, a street vendor protesting government corruption, sparked widespread outrage. Activists used social media to share his story, mobilizing protests that ultimately led to the overthrow of the government. Similarly, in Egypt, social media was used to organize massive demonstrations in Tahrir Square, which became a symbol of the revolution. Videos and photos shared online brought global attention to the protests, inspiring solidarity and support from people around the world.

Encrypted messaging apps, such as WhatsApp, Signal, and Telegram, have also become essential abilities for modern resistance movements. These platforms allow activists to communicate securely, protecting their messages from government surveillance and censorship. For example, during the 2019 protests in Hong Kong, activists used encrypted messaging apps to coordinate their actions and share real-time updates, ensuring that their efforts remained organized and effective. These abilities have empowered individuals and groups to challenge oppressive regimes, even in the face of significant risks.

Information networks have also been used to expose injustices and rally global support for social and political causes. Whistleblowers, journalists, and activists have used digital platforms to share evidence of corruption, human rights abuses, and environmental destruction, often at great personal risk. For example, the release of classified documents by whistleblowers like Edward Snowden and Chelsea Manning brought global attention to issues of government surveillance and military misconduct, sparking debates about privacy, accountability, and transparency.

However, the use of information networks for resistance and revolution is not without challenges and risks. Governments have developed sophisticated methods of surveillance and censorship to monitor and suppress dissent. In countries like China, the "Great Firewall" blocks access to foreign websites and censors online content, making it difficult for activists to share information or organize protests. Similarly, authoritarian regimes often use spyware and hacking to infiltrate activist networks, exposing individuals to arrest and persecution.

The spread of misinformation is another significant challenge. While information networks can be used to share accurate and reliable information, they can also be exploited to spread falsehoods and sow confusion. In some cases, governments and other actors have used disinformation campaigns to undermine resistance movements, discredit activists, and manipulate public opinion. This highlights the need for critical thinking and media literacy in the digital age, as individuals must navigate a complex and often unreliable information landscape.

Despite these challenges, information networks remain a powerful ability for resistance and revolution. They have empowered individuals and groups to challenge oppressive regimes, expose injustices, and rally global support for change. From the underground printing presses of the past to the encrypted messaging apps of today, these networks have demonstrated the enduring power of communication in the fight for freedom and justice.

Chapter 10

Algorithms And The Flow Of Information

Algorithms are everywhere in modern life, quietly working behind the scenes to make decisions, solve problems, and organize the vast amounts of information we interact with every day. While the term might sound technical or intimidating, the concept of an algorithm is actually quite simple. At its core, an algorithm is a set of step-by-step instructions or rules designed to perform a task or solve a problem. Think of it as a recipe in a cookbook: the recipe provides clear steps to follow in order to bake a cake. Similarly, algorithms provide instructions for computers to process data and complete tasks.

For example, imagine you're giving someone directions to your house. You might say, "Turn left at the first traffic light, go straight for two blocks, then turn right at the gas station." This is an algorithm—a sequence of steps that leads to a specific outcome. In the digital world, algorithms work in much the same way, but instead of guiding someone to a destination, they guide computers to process information, make decisions, or deliver results.

In modern information networks, algorithms play a crucial role in organizing and processing the enormous amounts of data generated every second. They are the invisible engines that power search engines, social media platforms, recommendation systems, and countless other technologies. For instance, when you type a question into Google, its search algorithm analyzes billions of web pages in a fraction of a second to deliver the most relevant results. This algorithm follows a set of rules to determine which pages are most likely to answer your question, taking into account factors like keywords, page quality, and user behavior.

Social media platforms like Facebook, Instagram, and Twitter also rely heavily on algorithms to decide what content appears in your feed. These algorithms analyze your past interactions—such as the posts you've liked, the accounts you follow, and the time you spend on certain types of content—to predict what you're most likely to engage with. For example, Facebook's News Feed algorithm prioritizes posts from friends, groups, or pages you interact with most often, ensuring that your feed feels personalized and relevant to you.

Recommendation systems, like those used by Netflix, Spotify, and Amazon, are another example of algorithms in action. These systems analyze your viewing, listening, or shopping history to suggest movies, songs, or products you might enjoy. If you've ever seen a "Because you watched…" section on Netflix or a "Customers who bought this also bought…" suggestion on Amazon, you've experienced the work of a recommendation algorithm. These systems make it easier to discover new content or products that match your preferences, saving you time and effort.

The benefits of algorithms are undeniable. They make complex tasks more efficient, allowing systems to process and analyze vast amounts of data at incredible speeds. They enable scalability, meaning they can handle millions—or even billions—of users simultaneously. And they provide personalized experiences, tailoring content, recommendations, and services to individual preferences. Without algorithms, navigating the internet or using modern digital services would be overwhelming and chaotic.

However, the widespread use of algorithms also comes with challenges and controversies. One major concern is bias. Algorithms are created by humans, and the data they rely on often reflects human biases. For example, if a hiring algorithm is trained on historical data that favors certain demographics, it may unintentionally discriminate against others. This has raised important questions about fairness and accountability in algorithmic decision-making.

Another issue is the lack of transparency. Many algorithms, especially those used by large tech companies, operate as "black boxes," meaning their inner workings are not visible to the public. Users often have no way of knowing how decisions are being made or why certain content is being prioritized. This lack of transparency can lead to mistrust and make it difficult to hold companies accountable for the impact of their algorithms.

Algorithms have also been criticized for their role in creating echo chambers and amplifying misinformation. On social media platforms, algorithms prioritize content that generates engagement, such as likes, shares, and comments. Unfortunately, this often means that sensational, emotionally charged, or polarizing content is amplified, as it tends to attract more attention. This can lead to the spread of misinformation and the formation of echo chambers, where users are exposed only to information that reinforces their existing beliefs. These dynamics can contribute to societal polarization and undermine trust in information networks.

Despite these challenges, algorithms remain an essential part of modern networks, and their potential for positive impact is immense. They have revolutionized how we access information, connect with others, and discover new content. At the same time, addressing the ethical and societal implications of algorithms is crucial to ensuring that they serve the greater good. This includes developing more transparent and accountable systems, reducing bias, and finding ways to balance personalization with the need for diverse perspectives.

The Benefits of Algorithms

Algorithms are the invisible engines driving much of the modern world, transforming how we live, work, and interact with technology. These step-by-step instructions, designed to solve problems and perform tasks, have brought remarkable benefits to society. By improving efficiency, enabling personalization, and driving innovation, algorithms have become essential to countless fields, from healthcare and entertainment to transportation and scientific research. Their ability to process vast amounts of data, automate complex tasks, and adapt to individual needs has revolutionized modern life, making it faster, smarter, and more connected.

One of the most significant benefits of algorithms is their ability to improve efficiency. In a world where vast amounts of data are generated every second, algorithms help us make sense of it all, automating tasks that would otherwise take humans hours, days, or even years to complete. For example, in logistics, algorithms are used to optimize supply chains, ensuring that goods are transported from manufacturers to consumers as quickly and cost-effectively as possible. Companies like Amazon rely on algorithms to manage their massive inventory, predict demand, and determine the fastest delivery routes. These systems save time, reduce costs, and ensure that customers receive their orders promptly.

In the financial sector, algorithms have revolutionized how transactions are processed and investments are managed. High-frequency trading algorithms, for instance, can analyze market trends and execute trades in milliseconds, far faster than any human could. This speed and precision allow financial institutions to maximize profits and minimize risks. Similarly, algorithms are used in fraud detection, analyzing patterns in transaction data to identify suspicious activity and protect consumers from financial crimes.

Healthcare is another field where algorithms have greatly improved efficiency. Medical algorithms assist doctors in diagnosing diseases, analyzing medical images, and recommending treatments. For example, algorithms powered by artificial intelligence (AI) can examine X-rays or MRIs to detect conditions like cancer or fractures with remarkable accuracy. These abilities not only save time but also improve patient outcomes by identifying issues that might be missed by the human eye. In public health, algorithms are used to track the spread of diseases, predict outbreaks, and allocate resources effectively, as seen during the COVID-19 pandemic.

Beyond efficiency, algorithms have transformed how we interact with technology by enabling personalization. In today's digital world, people expect experiences that are tailored to their individual preferences, and algorithms make this possible. Platforms like Netflix, Spotify, and Amazon use recommendation algorithms to suggest movies, music, or products based on a user's past behavior. For example, if you watch a lot of action movies on Netflix, the platform's algorithm will suggest similar films you might enjoy. This personalization creates a more engaging and satisfying experience, helping users discover content that matches their tastes.

Personalization extends beyond entertainment and shopping. Social media platforms like Facebook, Instagram, and Twitter use algorithms to curate users' feeds, showing posts and updates that are most relevant to them. While this can make social media more enjoyable, it also highlights the power of algorithms to shape what we see and interact with online. In education, personalized learning platforms use algorithms to adapt lessons to each student's needs, helping them learn at their own pace and focus on areas where they need the most improvement.

Perhaps the most exciting benefit of algorithms is their role in driving innovation. By powering advancements in artificial intelligence, robotics, and scientific research, algorithms are opening up new possibilities and solving problems that were once thought to be insurmountable. Self-driving cars, for example, rely on complex algorithms to process data from sensors, cameras, and GPS systems, allowing them to navigate roads, avoid obstacles, and make decisions in real time. These vehicles have the potential to reduce traffic accidents, improve fuel efficiency, and transform transportation as we know it.

In the field of natural language processing, algorithms enable technologies like virtual assistants (e.g., Siri, Alexa, and Google Assistant) to understand and respond to human speech. These systems use algorithms to analyze language, recognize patterns, and generate appropriate responses, making it easier for people to interact with technology in a natural and intuitive way. Similarly, algorithms power translation abilities like Google Translate, breaking down language barriers and facilitating global communication.

Scientific research has also been revolutionized by algorithms. In climate science, algorithms are used to model complex systems, predict weather patterns, and study the impacts of climate change. These models help scientists understand how the planet is changing and develop strategies to mitigate its effects. In medicine, algorithms are accelerating drug discovery by analyzing vast datasets to identify potential treatments for diseases. For example, during the COVID-19 pandemic, algorithms were used to analyze the virus's genetic structure and identify potential vaccine candidates, speeding up the development process and saving lives.

While the benefits of algorithms are undeniable, it is important to recognize that their impact depends on how they are designed and used. When implemented responsibly, algorithms can improve efficiency, enhance personalization, and drive innovation in ways that benefit society as a whole. However, as algorithms become more integrated into our lives, it is essential to address challenges such as bias, transparency, and ethical considerations to ensure that their benefits are distributed fairly and equitably.

The Risks of Algorithms

Algorithms have become a powerful force in modern life, shaping decisions that affect everything from the ads we see online to the loans we qualify for and even the jobs we are offered. While they bring many benefits, such as efficiency and innovation, algorithms also come with significant risks. Issues like bias, lack of transparency, and accountability have raised serious concerns about how algorithms are designed, implemented, and used. These risks highlight the need for careful oversight and ethical considerations to ensure that algorithms serve society fairly and responsibly.

One of the most pressing risks of algorithms is bias. Algorithms are not inherently neutral; they are created by humans and rely on data to function. If the data used to train an algorithm contains biases—whether intentional or unintentional—the algorithm can replicate and even amplify those biases. For example, hiring algorithms designed to screen job applicants have been found to favor men over women because they were trained on historical hiring data that reflected gender biases in the workplace. Instead of promoting fairness, these algorithms reinforced existing inequalities.

Facial recognition systems provide another striking example of algorithmic bias. Studies have shown that some facial recognition algorithms are significantly less accurate at identifying people with darker skin tones compared to those with lighter skin tones. This has led to real-world consequences, such as wrongful arrests and discrimination, particularly against people of color. These inaccuracies stem from biased training data that underrepresents certain groups, highlighting how the quality and diversity of data play a critical role in algorithmic fairness.

Discriminatory lending practices are yet another example of how bias in algorithms can harm individuals. Some financial algorithms used to determine creditworthiness have been found to disadvantage minority groups, even when race is not explicitly included as a factor. This happens because the algorithms rely on other data points, such as zip codes or income levels, which can serve as proxies for race or socioeconomic status. As a result, people from marginalized communities may be unfairly denied loans or charged higher interest rates, perpetuating cycles of inequality.

The issue of transparency is closely tied to the problem of bias. Many algorithms operate as "black boxes," meaning their inner workings are not easily understood by users—or even by the people who created them. This lack of transparency makes it difficult to identify errors, biases, or unfair outcomes. For example, social media algorithms prioritize content that generates engagement, such as likes, shares, and comments. While this can make platforms more engaging, it can also amplify harmful content, such as misinformation, hate speech, or divisive posts. Users often have no way of knowing why certain content appears in their feeds, leading to mistrust and concerns about the impact of these algorithms on public discourse.

Credit scoring systems are another area where transparency is a major concern. These algorithms determine whether someone qualifies for a loan or credit card, yet the criteria they use are often unclear. If a person is denied credit, they may not understand why or how to improve their chances in the future. This lack of clarity can lead to frustration and a sense of unfairness, particularly when the decisions have significant consequences for people's financial well-being.

Transparency is also critical in high-stakes areas like healthcare and criminal justice. For instance, algorithms used to predict patient outcomes or assess the risk of reoffending in criminal cases can have life-altering impacts. If these algorithms are not transparent, it becomes nearly impossible to evaluate their accuracy or fairness. This raises important questions about whether we can trust algorithms to make decisions that affect people's lives.

The third major risk of algorithms is accountability. When an algorithm causes harm or makes an unethical decision, it is often unclear who should be held responsible. Is it the developer who designed the algorithm? The company that deployed it? Or the government agency that approved its use? This lack of accountability creates a gray area where no one takes responsibility for the consequences of algorithmic decisions.

For example, if a self-driving car powered by algorithms causes an accident, who is at fault? Is it the car manufacturer, the software developer, or the owner of the vehicle? These questions highlight the ethical and legal challenges of holding individuals or organizations accountable for the actions of algorithms. Without clear accountability, there is little incentive for companies to address the risks associated with their algorithms, leaving users vulnerable to harm.

The issue of accountability is further complicated by the global nature of algorithms. Many algorithms are developed and deployed across borders, making it difficult to establish consistent regulations or enforce ethical standards. For instance, a social media platform based in one country may use algorithms that influence elections or spread misinformation in another. This raises questions about who is responsible for regulating these algorithms and ensuring they are used responsibly.

To address these risks, it is essential to develop regulations, ethical guidelines, and oversight mechanisms that promote fairness, transparency, and accountability in algorithmic systems. This includes requiring companies to audit their algorithms for bias, disclose how they work, and provide explanations for their decisions. It also means holding organizations accountable when their algorithms cause harm, whether through legal frameworks or industry standards.

In addition, fostering public awareness and education about algorithms is crucial. People need to understand how algorithms affect their lives and be equipped to question their fairness and accuracy. This can empower individuals to advocate for greater transparency and accountability, ensuring that algorithms are used in ways that benefit society as a whole.

How Algorithms Shape Our Choices and Behaviors

In today's digital world, algorithms have become powerful abilities that influence nearly every aspect of our lives. From the content we see on social media to the products we buy online, algorithms are constantly working behind the scenes to shape our choices and behaviors. These step-by-step instructions, designed to analyze data and predict preferences, are not just passive abilities—they actively guide how we interact with the world, often in ways we don't even realize. By tailoring content, recommendations, and advertisements to individual users, algorithms have a profound impact on our decision-making, our habits, and even our beliefs.

At their core, algorithms are designed to process vast amounts of data and make predictions. When you use a social media platform, shop online, or stream a movie, algorithms analyze your behavior— what you click on, how long you watch something, what you like or share—and use this information to predict what you might want to see or do next. For example, when you open Netflix, its recommendation algorithm suggests movies and TV shows based on your viewing history and the preferences of users with similar tastes. Similarly, Amazon's algorithm recommends products you might be interested in, while Spotify curates playlists tailored to your music preferences. These personalized experiences make it easier to find content or products that match your interests, but they also subtly guide your choices by prioritizing certain options over others.

Social media platforms like Facebook, Instagram, TikTok, and YouTube take this personalization to another level. Their algorithms are designed to maximize engagement, meaning they prioritize content that is most likely to keep you scrolling, liking, and sharing. For example, TikTok's "For You" page uses an algorithm to show videos that match your interests, based on how you interact with the app. If you spend more time watching funny videos or dance challenges, the algorithm will show you more of that type of content. Similarly, YouTube's recommendation algorithm suggests videos that align with your viewing history, encouraging you to keep watching for hours.

While these algorithms make platforms more engaging, they also have significant psychological and behavioral effects. One of the most notable effects is the creation of echo chambers, where users are exposed primarily to content that reinforces their existing beliefs. For example, if you frequently watch videos or read posts about a particular political viewpoint, the algorithm will show you more content that aligns with that perspective. Over time, this can limit your exposure to diverse opinions and create a distorted view of reality, as you only see information that confirms what you already believe.

Algorithms can also reinforce biases, both at an individual and societal level. For instance, if an algorithm is trained on biased data, it may perpetuate stereotypes or discriminatory practices. This is particularly concerning in areas like hiring, lending, or law enforcement, where algorithmic decisions can have real-world consequences. Even in everyday interactions, algorithms can subtly shape how we think and behave by amplifying certain ideas or trends while suppressing others.

Another significant effect of algorithmic influence is the encouragement of addictive behaviors. Social media platforms, in particular, are designed to keep users engaged for as long as possible. Features like infinite scrolling, autoplay, and notifications are all driven by algorithms that analyze user behavior and optimize for maximum time spent on the platform. This can lead to compulsive use, as users feel compelled to keep checking their feeds or watching "just one more" video. Over time, this can affect mental health, leading to feelings of anxiety, stress, or dissatisfaction.

The influence of algorithms extends beyond individual behavior to broader societal trends. For example, algorithms play a significant role in shaping public opinion by determining what information people see and how it is presented. During elections, political campaigns use algorithms to target ads to specific groups of voters, tailoring messages to their interests and concerns. While this can be an effective way to engage voters, it also raises concerns about manipulation and the spread of misinformation. Targeted ads can exploit people's fears or biases, influencing their decisions in ways they may not fully understand.

Filter bubbles, created by algorithms that prioritize personalized content, can also contribute to societal polarization. When people are exposed only to information that aligns with their beliefs, it becomes harder to find common ground or engage in constructive dialogue. This can deepen divisions within society, as different groups become more entrenched in their perspectives and less willing to consider alternative viewpoints.

Algorithms also play a role in amplifying misinformation, particularly on social media platforms. Content that is sensational, emotionally charged, or controversial tends to generate more engagement, which means algorithms are more likely to prioritize it. This can lead to the rapid spread of false or misleading information, with serious consequences for public trust and decision-making. For example, during the COVID-19 pandemic, misinformation about the virus, vaccines, and treatments spread widely on social media, complicating efforts to combat the crisis and protect public health.

Despite these challenges, algorithms are not inherently good or bad—they are abilities that reflect the goals and values of the people who design and use them. When used responsibly, algorithms can enhance our lives by making information more accessible, improving efficiency, and creating personalized experiences. However, their influence on our choices and behaviors also highlights the need for greater transparency, accountability, and ethical considerations in their design and implementation.

Chapter 11

Will Technology Bring Us Together or Tear Us Apart?

The Role of Technology in Breaking Down Barriers

Technology has always been a driving force for progress, breaking down barriers that once seemed insurmountable. From connecting people across vast distances to empowering marginalized communities and creating new economic opportunities, technological advancements have transformed the way we live, work, and interact with the world. By overcoming physical, social, and economic barriers, technology has fostered greater connectivity and inclusivity, making the world more accessible and equitable for millions of people.

One of the most remarkable ways technology has broken down barriers is by bridging geographic distances. Innovations like the internet, smartphones, and communication platforms have made it possible for people to connect and collaborate across the globe in real time. In the past, communicating with someone on the other side of the world required letters that took weeks to arrive or expensive long-distance phone calls. Today, video conferencing abilities like Zoom, Microsoft Teams, and Google Meet allow people to hold face-to-face conversations instantly, no matter where they are. This has revolutionized industries, enabling remote work and global collaboration. For example, a software developer in India can work seamlessly with a team in the United States, while a teacher in Australia can deliver lessons to students in Africa.

Online education is another powerful example of how technology has made the world more accessible. Platforms like Coursera, Khan Academy, and edX offer courses from top universities and institutions, allowing anyone with an internet connection to learn new skills or earn certifications. This has opened up educational opportunities for people in remote or underserved areas who might not have access to traditional schools or universities. Similarly, remote work, made possible by technology, has allowed people to pursue careers without being limited by their physical location. A graphic designer in a small town can now work for a company in a major city, breaking down the barriers of geography and creating new possibilities for employment.

Technology has also played a crucial role in breaking down social barriers, empowering marginalized communities, and amplifying diverse voices. Social media platforms like Twitter, Instagram, and TikTok have given individuals a platform to share their stories, advocate for change, and connect with others who share their experiences. Movements like #MeToo, #BlackLivesMatter, and #DisabilityPride have gained global attention through social media, raising awareness about social justice issues and inspiring collective action. These platforms have allowed people from all walks of life to participate in conversations that were once dominated by a select few, fostering greater inclusivity and representation.

Assistive technologies have further broken down social barriers by improving accessibility for people with disabilities. Innovations like screen readers, voice recognition software, and prosthetic devices have enabled individuals with disabilities to participate more fully in society. For example, screen readers allow visually impaired individuals to navigate the internet and access information, while voice recognition software enables people with mobility challenges to control devices and communicate more easily. These technologies have not only improved quality of life but also created opportunities for education, employment, and social interaction.

In addition to addressing physical and social barriers, technology has also tackled economic barriers, creating opportunities for entrepreneurship, access to global markets, and financial inclusion. E-commerce platforms like Amazon, Etsy, and Shopify have made it possible for small businesses and independent creators to reach customers around the world. A craftsperson in a rural village can now sell their products to buyers in urban centers or even internationally, bypassing traditional barriers like limited local demand or lack of access to physical marketplaces. This has empowered countless entrepreneurs to build businesses and improve their livelihoods.

Mobile banking and digital payment systems have been particularly transformative in developing countries, where access to traditional banking services is often limited. Platforms like M-Pesa in Kenya have enabled millions of people to send and receive money, pay bills, and access credit using their mobile phones. This has not only improved financial inclusion but also supported economic growth by making it easier for individuals and businesses to participate in the economy. For example, a farmer in a remote area can now receive payments for their produce directly to their mobile phone, eliminating the need for costly and time-consuming trips to the nearest bank.

Online learning abilities have also addressed economic barriers by providing affordable education to underserved populations. Platforms like Udemy and Skillshare offer low-cost courses on a wide range of topics, from coding and graphic design to business and marketing. These resources allow individuals to acquire new skills and improve their employability without the high costs associated with traditional education. In many cases, online learning has been a lifeline for people looking to adapt to changing job markets or start new careers.

While technology has made incredible strides in breaking down barriers, it is important to acknowledge that challenges remain. Digital inequality, for example, continues to limit access to technology for many people, particularly in rural or low-income areas. Ensuring that everyone can benefit from technological advancements requires ongoing efforts to expand internet access, provide affordable devices, and promote digital literacy.

Social Media and Global Movements: The Power of Connection

Social media has transformed the way people connect, communicate, and organize, becoming one of the most powerful abilities for global movements in the 21st century. Platforms like Twitter, Facebook, Instagram, and TikTok have broken down barriers of geography, language, and access, enabling individuals and groups to share information instantly, amplify their voices, and mobilize support for causes that matter to them. By democratizing communication, social media has given a voice to marginalized communities, empowered grassroots activism, and fostered solidarity across borders. It has become a digital stage where anyone, regardless of their background, can participate in shaping the world.

One of the most significant ways social media has empowered global movements is by connecting people across the globe in real time. In the past, organizing protests or raising awareness about an issue often required access to traditional media outlets like newspapers, radio, or television. These channels were controlled by gatekeepers who decided which stories were told and whose voices were heard. Social media has changed this dynamic entirely. Now, anyone with a smartphone and an internet connection can share their story, reach millions of people, and inspire action. This has made it possible for movements to grow rapidly, fueled by the power of connection and shared purpose.

The Arab Spring is a powerful example of how social media can ignite and sustain global movements. Beginning in late 2010, a wave of pro-democracy uprisings swept across the Middle East and North Africa, challenging authoritarian regimes and demanding political reform. Social media platforms like Facebook and Twitter played a central role in these uprisings, allowing activists to organize protests, share real-time updates, and document government crackdowns. In Egypt, for example, activists used Facebook to coordinate massive demonstrations in Tahrir Square, while Twitter became a platform for sharing news and rallying international support. Videos and photos posted on social media brought global attention to the struggles of ordinary citizens, inspiring solidarity and putting pressure on governments to respond.

Another example of social media's transformative power is the #MeToo movement, which began as a hashtag on Twitter in 2017 and quickly became a global phenomenon. The movement encouraged survivors of sexual harassment and assault to share their stories, breaking the silence around these issues and holding powerful individuals accountable. Social media provided a platform for survivors to connect, support one another, and amplify their voices, creating a ripple effect that reached industries, institutions, and governments worldwide. The #MeToo movement demonstrated how social media can empower individuals to challenge systemic injustices and demand change.

The Black Lives Matter (BLM) movement is another testament to the power of social media in driving global activism. Founded in 2013, BLM gained widespread attention in 2020 following the murder of George Floyd, a Black man killed by a police officer in the United States. Videos of the incident, shared on platforms like Facebook and Instagram, sparked outrage and mobilized millions of people around the world to demand racial justice and police reform. Hashtags like #BlackLivesMatter and #JusticeForGeorgeFloyd trended globally, uniting people from diverse backgrounds in a shared call for change. Social media not only helped organize protests but also provided a space for education, dialogue, and solidarity, making the movement a global force for racial equality.

Climate change activism has also been profoundly shaped by social media, with figures like Greta Thunberg using platforms like Twitter and Instagram to inspire a new generation of environmental advocates. Greta's #FridaysForFuture campaign, which began as a solo protest outside the Swedish parliament, grew into a global movement thanks to social media. Young people around the world used hashtags, shared photos of their climate strikes, and connected with one another to demand urgent action on climate change. Social media allowed these activists to bypass traditional media gatekeepers, spread their message directly to millions, and build a sense of global community.

The benefits of social media in fostering global movements are undeniable. It allows activists to bypass traditional barriers, share real-time updates, and create a sense of shared purpose. For example, during protests or natural disasters, social media can provide critical information about safe routes, meeting points, or emergency resources. It also amplifies voices that might otherwise go unheard, giving marginalized communities a platform to share their experiences and advocate for change. By connecting people from different backgrounds and regions, social media fosters empathy, understanding, and solidarity, making it possible to build coalitions that transcend borders.

However, the power of social media also comes with challenges and risks. One of the most significant challenges is the spread of misinformation. While social media can be a powerful ability for sharing accurate information, it can also amplify false or misleading content. During global movements, misinformation can sow confusion, undermine trust, and even put people's safety at risk. For example, during the COVID-19 pandemic, false information about the virus and vaccines spread widely on social media, complicating efforts to combat the crisis and protect public health.

Online harassment is another major risk associated with social media activism. Activists, particularly those from marginalized communities, often face targeted harassment, threats, and abuse online. This can create a hostile environment that discourages participation and silences voices that are critical to the movement. For example, women and LGBTQ+ activists frequently report experiencing online harassment, which can take a significant emotional and psychological toll.

Governments and corporations also have the ability to suppress or manipulate online activism. In some cases, governments have shut down internet access or blocked social media platforms to prevent activists from organizing or sharing information. For example, during protests in Myanmar in 2021, the military government imposed internet blackouts to stifle dissent. Corporations, too, can influence online activism by controlling algorithms that determine what content is seen and by whom. This raises important questions about the role of tech companies in shaping public discourse and the need for greater transparency and accountability.

The Rise of Echo Chambers and Polarization

In the digital age, the way we consume information has changed dramatically. Social media platforms, search engines, and other digital abilities have made it easier than ever to access news, opinions, and ideas. But this convenience comes with a hidden cost: the rise of echo chambers and polarization. Echo chambers are environments where individuals are primarily exposed to information and opinions that align with their existing beliefs, while opposing viewpoints are filtered out or ignored. These echo chambers, often fueled by algorithms and human psychology, have contributed to growing divisions in society, making it harder for people to engage in meaningful dialogue or find common ground.

At the heart of echo chambers are the algorithms that power digital platforms. Social media platforms like Facebook, Twitter, and YouTube use algorithms to decide what content to show users.

These algorithms are designed to maximize engagement—likes, shares, comments, and time spent on the platform. To achieve this, they prioritize content that aligns with a user's preferences and past behavior. For example, if someone frequently interacts with posts about a particular political party or ideology, the algorithm will show them more content that supports that perspective. Over time, this creates a feedback loop where users are exposed to a narrow range of ideas, reinforcing their existing beliefs and filtering out opposing viewpoints.

This process is not inherently malicious; it is simply how algorithms are designed to keep users engaged. However, the unintended consequence is the creation of echo chambers, where people are surrounded by like-minded perspectives. In these spaces, individuals are less likely to encounter diverse viewpoints or challenge their assumptions. Instead, they are presented with information that confirms what they already believe, making their views more rigid and less open to change.

The impact of echo chambers extends beyond individual users; it has profound effects on society as a whole. One of the most concerning consequences is polarization—the deepening of ideological divides between groups with opposing beliefs. In polarized societies, people are less willing to listen to or understand those who hold different opinions. Instead, they view those on the "other side" as adversaries or even enemies. This dynamic has been observed in various contexts, such as political polarization in the United States. For example, during recent elections, social media platforms became battlegrounds for partisan content, with users on the left and right consuming entirely different narratives about the same events. This division has made it increasingly difficult for people to engage in civil discourse or work together to address shared challenges.

The Brexit debates in the United Kingdom provide another example of how echo chambers can influence public opinion and societal cohesion. During the lead-up to the 2016 referendum on whether the UK should leave the European Union, social media platforms were flooded with targeted ads, memes, and articles tailored to specific audiences. Pro-Brexit and anti-Brexit groups operated in separate echo chambers, each consuming content that reinforced their stance. This lack of exposure to opposing viewpoints contributed to a highly polarized and emotionally charged debate, leaving the country deeply divided even after the referendum.

Echo chambers also play a significant role in the spread of conspiracy theories. When individuals join online communities that share their beliefs, they are more likely to encounter and accept misinformation that aligns with their worldview. For example, conspiracy theories about vaccines, climate change, or election fraud often gain traction in echo chambers where skepticism of mainstream information is already high. These theories can spread rapidly within these closed networks, influencing public opinion and undermining trust in institutions.

The appeal of echo chambers lies in human psychology. People are naturally drawn to information that confirms their beliefs, a phenomenon known as confirmation bias. Engaging with like-minded communities provides a sense of validation and belonging, making individuals feel more confident in their views. This comfort can be especially appealing in a world that often feels complex and uncertain. However, the downside is that it discourages critical thinking and open-mindedness, as people become less willing to question their assumptions or consider alternative perspectives.

The risks of polarization fueled by echo chambers are significant. One major concern is the erosion of civil discourse—the ability to have respectful and constructive conversations with those who hold different opinions. In polarized societies, discussions often devolve into arguments or personal attacks, making it harder to address important issues collaboratively. This breakdown in communication can lead to gridlock in politics, where opposing sides are unable to compromise or find solutions to pressing problems.

Another risk is the spread of misinformation. In echo chambers, false or misleading information can go unchallenged, as users are less likely to encounter fact-checks or alternative viewpoints. This can have serious consequences, from undermining public health efforts to influencing elections. For example, during the COVID-19 pandemic, misinformation about the virus and vaccines spread widely on social media, fueled by echo chambers where skepticism of science and authority was already prevalent. This misinformation not only endangered lives but also deepened divisions between those who trusted public health guidance and those who did not.

Finally, polarization makes it harder to find common ground on critical issues. Whether it's climate change, economic inequality, or social justice, addressing complex challenges requires collaboration and mutual understanding. Echo chambers, by isolating people in ideological silos, make it harder to build the trust and empathy needed to work together. Instead, they foster an "us versus them" mentality that hinders progress and exacerbates divisions.

Addressing Misinformation and Digital Inequality

In the digital age, information is more accessible than ever before, but this accessibility comes with significant challenges. Misinformation and digital inequality are two of the most pressing issues facing society today. Misinformation spreads rapidly through social media platforms, search engines, and other digital networks, often distorting facts and influencing public opinion in harmful ways. At the same time, digital inequality—the unequal access to technology and the internet—creates barriers for millions of people, limiting their ability to participate fully in the modern world. These challenges are deeply interconnected, and addressing them requires collective action from governments, tech companies, and civil society.

Misinformation thrives in the digital world because of how information is shared and consumed online. Social media platforms and search engines use algorithms to prioritize content that generates engagement—likes, shares, and comments. Unfortunately, sensational or emotionally charged content often attracts more attention than accurate or balanced information. As a result, false or misleading content can spread quickly, reaching millions of people before it is corrected or debunked. This phenomenon has been observed in various contexts, from elections to public health crises.

For example, during the COVID-19 pandemic, misinformation about the virus, vaccines, and treatments spread widely on social media. False claims, such as the idea that vaccines contained microchips or that certain unproven remedies could cure the virus, led to confusion and mistrust. This misinformation undermined public health efforts, making it harder to control the spread of the virus and protect vulnerable populations. Similarly, during elections, fake news and conspiracy theories have been used to manipulate voters, sow division, and undermine trust in democratic institutions. These examples highlight the real-world consequences of misinformation, which can harm individuals, communities, and society as a whole.

While misinformation affects everyone, its impact is often amplified by digital inequality. Digital inequality refers to the gap between those who have access to technology and the internet and those who do not. This gap is shaped by factors such as income, education, geography, and infrastructure. For example, people in rural areas or developing countries may lack reliable internet access, while low-income families may struggle to afford devices like smartphones or laptops. Digital inequality also affects marginalized communities, who may face additional barriers to accessing technology due to systemic discrimination or lack of resources.

The consequences of digital inequality are far-reaching. Without access to technology and the internet, individuals are excluded from opportunities in education, employment, and civic participation. For example, students in underserved areas may struggle to access online learning resources, putting them at a disadvantage compared to their peers. Similarly, small businesses without internet access may miss out on opportunities to reach customers or compete in the global marketplace. Digital inequality also limits access to reliable information, making it harder for people to identify and counter misinformation. This creates a vicious cycle, where those who are most vulnerable to misinformation are also the least equipped to combat it.

Addressing misinformation and digital inequality requires a multi-faceted approach. One of the most effective ways to combat misinformation is by promoting digital literacy. Digital literacy involves teaching people how to critically evaluate information, recognize credible sources, and identify false or misleading content. Schools, community organizations, and governments can play a key role in providing digital literacy education, equipping individuals with the skills they need to navigate the digital world responsibly.

Fact-checking initiatives are another important strategy for addressing misinformation. Organizations like Snopes, FactCheck.org, and PolitiFact work to verify the accuracy of claims and provide reliable information to the public. Social media platforms can also play a role by partnering with fact-checkers to flag or remove false content. For example, during the COVID-19 pandemic, platforms like Facebook and Twitter implemented measures to label or remove posts containing misinformation about the virus. While these efforts are not perfect, they represent an important step toward reducing the spread of false information.

Holding tech companies accountable for the content they amplify is also crucial. Platforms must take responsibility for the role their algorithms play in spreading misinformation and prioritize accuracy over engagement. This could involve adjusting algorithms to promote credible sources, increasing transparency about how content is prioritized, and providing users with abilities to report or challenge false information. Governments and regulators can support these efforts by establishing clear guidelines and standards for content moderation, ensuring that platforms act in the public interest.

Addressing digital inequality requires a different set of solutions, focused on expanding access to technology and the internet. One of the most important steps is investing in infrastructure to bring reliable internet access to underserved areas, such as rural communities and developing countries. Governments and private companies can work together to build broadband networks, provide affordable internet plans, and ensure that no one is left behind in the digital age.

Providing affordable devices is another key strategy. Programs that distribute low-cost laptops, tablets, or smartphones to low-income families can help bridge the digital divide and ensure that everyone has the abilities they need to participate in the digital world. For example, initiatives like the One Laptop Per Child program have provided millions of children in developing countries with access to technology, opening up new opportunities for education and learning.

Investing in digital education programs is equally important. These programs can teach individuals how to use technology effectively, from basic skills like navigating the internet to more advanced abilities like coding or data analysis. By empowering people with digital skills, these programs can help close the gap between those who have access to technology and those who do not, creating a more inclusive and equitable society.

Collaboration is essential to tackling these interconnected challenges. Governments, tech companies, and civil society must work together to develop and implement solutions that address both misinformation and digital inequality. For example, governments can provide funding and policy support for digital inclusion initiatives, while tech companies can invest in abilities and features that promote accurate information and reduce the spread of false content. Civil society organizations can play a critical role in advocating for change, raising awareness, and providing education and resources to communities in need.

Balancing Digital and Real-World Interactions

In today's world, digital technologies have become an integral part of how we connect, communicate, and build relationships. Social media platforms, messaging apps, and virtual meeting abilities have transformed the way we interact, making it easier than ever to stay in touch with friends, family, and colleagues, no matter where they are. These technologies have brought incredible benefits, allowing us to maintain relationships across distances, collaborate with people around the globe, and share moments of our lives instantly. However, as our reliance on digital communication grows, it is becoming increasingly important to find a balance between our online interactions and our real-world relationships.

Digital communication has revolutionized the way we connect with others. Platforms like WhatsApp, Facebook, Instagram, and Zoom allow us to communicate instantly, breaking down barriers of time and distance. For example, a family separated by thousands of miles can stay connected through video calls, sharing their lives in real time. Friends can maintain close bonds through group chats, even if they live in different cities or countries. Social media enables us to share updates, photos, and experiences with a wide audience, helping us feel connected to others even when we are apart. These abilities have been especially valuable during times of crisis, such as the COVID-19 pandemic, when physical distancing made in-person interactions difficult or impossible.

The convenience and accessibility of digital communication have also opened up new opportunities for global connectivity. People can now form relationships and collaborate with others across cultures and continents, creating a more interconnected world. For example, virtual meetings and online communities allow professionals to work together on projects without needing to be in the same physical location. Social media has also given rise to online communities where people with shared interests or experiences can connect, support one another, and build meaningful relationships.

Despite these benefits, excessive reliance on digital interactions can pose significant challenges. One of the most concerning issues is the potential for social isolation. While digital communication can help us stay connected, it can also create a false sense of closeness. For example, liking a friend's post on Instagram or sending a quick text message may feel like meaningful interaction, but it often lacks the depth and emotional connection of face-to-face conversations. Over time, this can lead to feelings of loneliness and disconnection, as digital interactions replace more meaningful, in-person connections.

Another challenge is the impact of digital communication on face-to-face social skills. As people spend more time communicating through screens, they may become less comfortable with in-person interactions. For example, younger generations who have grown up with smartphones and social media may struggle with skills like reading body language, maintaining eye contact, or engaging in deep, meaningful conversations. This decline in face-to-face communication skills can make it harder to build strong, authentic relationships in the real world.

The rise of "screen time" concerns also highlights the potential negative effects of excessive digital use on mental health. Social media, in particular, has been linked to issues like low self-esteem, anxiety, and depression. Platforms like Instagram and TikTok often present an idealized version of reality, where people share only the highlights of their lives. This can create unrealistic expectations and lead to feelings of inadequacy or comparison. For example, someone scrolling through photos of friends on vacation or achieving milestones may feel like their own life is less exciting or successful, even if this is not true.

Excessive screen time can also interfere with real-world relationships and experiences. For example, it is common to see people at social gatherings glued to their phones, checking notifications or scrolling through social media instead of engaging with the people around them. This lack of presence can weaken relationships and prevent people from fully enjoying the moment. Over time, it can create a sense of disconnection, even in situations where people are physically together.

To address these challenges, it is essential to find a healthy balance between digital and real-world interactions. One effective strategy is setting boundaries for screen time. For example, individuals can establish "tech-free" zones or times, such as during meals, family gatherings, or before bed. This creates opportunities to focus on real-world connections and activities without the distraction of digital devices. Many smartphones now include features that track screen time and allow users to set limits on app usage, making it easier to manage digital habits.

Prioritizing in-person connections is another important step. While digital communication is convenient, it should not replace face-to-face interactions. Making time for activities like meeting friends for coffee, attending social events, or spending quality time with family can help strengthen relationships and create deeper connections. For example, instead of texting a friend to catch up, consider inviting them to meet in person. These real-world interactions provide opportunities for meaningful conversations, shared experiences, and emotional connection that cannot be fully replicated online.

Using technology mindfully is also key to achieving balance. This means being intentional about how and why we use digital abilities, rather than letting them dictate our behavior. For example, instead of mindlessly scrolling through social media, individuals can use these platforms to enhance their real-world relationships, such as by organizing events, sharing important updates, or staying in touch with distant loved ones. Mindful use of technology also involves being aware of its impact on our mental health and taking steps to address any negative effects, such as limiting exposure to content that triggers comparison or anxiety.

Ultimately, balancing digital and real-world interactions is about fostering meaningful relationships and maintaining a sense of presence in the physical world. While digital communication has its benefits, it should complement, not replace, real-world connections. By setting boundaries, prioritizing in-person interactions, and using technology mindfully, we can enjoy the advantages of digital abilities while preserving the richness and depth of our real-world relationships.

Chapter 12

Emerging Technologies And The Future Of Communication

Artificial Intelligence

Artificial intelligence (AI) has become a transformative force in the way ideas are shared, communicated, and amplified. By automating tasks, personalizing communication, and breaking down barriers, AI has opened up new opportunities for individuals and organizations to express themselves and connect with others. At the same time, the rapid growth of AI has introduced challenges and ethical concerns that must be addressed to ensure it is used responsibly. The balance between these opportunities and challenges defines AI's role in shaping the future of how we share ideas.

One of the most exciting opportunities AI provides is its ability to automate content creation. Abilities like ChatGPT, DALL·E, and other AI-powered systems can generate text, images, and even videos, making it easier for people to bring their ideas to life. For example, a writer can use AI to draft an article, refine their language, or brainstorm creative concepts. Similarly, businesses can use AI to create marketing materials, social media posts, or customer support responses, saving time and resources. This automation allows individuals and organizations to focus on the creative and strategic aspects of their work, while AI handles repetitive or time-consuming tasks.

AI also enhances the personalization of communication, tailoring messages to individual preferences and needs. Recommendation systems, like those used by Netflix, Spotify, and YouTube, analyze user behavior to suggest content that aligns with their interests. This personalization helps people discover new ideas, stories, and perspectives that resonate with them. In education, AI-powered platforms like Duolingo and Khan Academy adapt lessons to each student's learning pace, making it easier for learners to grasp complex concepts and stay engaged. By delivering content that feels relevant and meaningful, AI fosters deeper connections between people and the ideas they encounter.

Another remarkable ability of AI is its role in breaking down language barriers. Real-time translation abilities, such as Google Translate and AI-powered transcription services, enable people from different linguistic backgrounds to communicate and collaborate seamlessly. For example, a business in Japan can use AI to translate its marketing materials into multiple languages, reaching a global audience. Similarly, international teams can use AI to facilitate meetings and discussions, ensuring that language differences do not hinder the sharing of ideas. This ability to connect people across cultures and languages has democratized access to information, making it possible for ideas to travel farther and faster than ever before.

AI's ability to analyze vast amounts of data has also revolutionized how ideas are shared and understood. In journalism, for instance, AI can sift through large datasets to uncover trends, patterns, and insights that would be difficult for humans to identify. This has led to more data-driven reporting, helping journalists tell stories that are both accurate and impactful. In the creative industries, AI abilities like Adobe Sensei assist designers and artists by suggesting edits, generating ideas, and streamlining workflows. These abilities empower individuals and organizations to share their ideas more effectively, reaching wider audiences and making a greater impact.

However, alongside these opportunities, AI also presents significant challenges in the sharing of ideas. One of the most pressing concerns is the spread of misinformation. AI can generate content that appears highly credible, making it easier for false information to spread. For example, deepfake technology can create realistic videos of people saying or doing things they never actually did, which can be used to manipulate public opinion or damage reputations. Similarly, AI-generated fake news articles can be shared widely on social media, misleading readers and distorting the truth. These risks highlight the need for vigilance and critical thinking when consuming AI-generated content.

Another challenge is the ethical implications of AI in communication. Bias in algorithms is a major concern, as AI systems often reflect the biases present in the data they are trained on. For example, an AI-powered hiring ability might favor certain candidates over others based on biased training data, perpetuating inequalities. In the context of sharing ideas, biased algorithms can amplify certain voices while silencing others, creating an uneven playing field. This raises important questions about fairness, representation, and accountability in the use of AI.

The loss of human authenticity in communication is another issue to consider. While AI can generate content that is polished and professional, it may lack the emotional depth and personal touch that come from human expression. For example, an AI-generated poem or story might be technically impressive but fail to capture the unique perspective and creativity of a human author. This raises concerns about the role of AI in creative fields and the value we place on human originality.

Over-reliance on AI systems is also a potential risk. As AI becomes more integrated into our lives, there is a danger that people may become too dependent on these abilities, losing critical skills and judgment. For example, if students rely solely on AI to complete their assignments, they may miss out on the opportunity to develop their own writing and analytical abilities. Similarly, if businesses rely too heavily on AI for decision-making, they may overlook important human factors, such as empathy and intuition.

To address these challenges, it is essential to establish transparency, accountability, and ethical guidelines for the use of AI in sharing ideas. Transparency involves making it clear when content is AI-generated and providing information about how algorithms work. For example, social media platforms could label AI-generated posts or explain how their recommendation systems prioritize content. Accountability means holding developers, companies, and users responsible for the impact of AI systems, ensuring that they are used in ways that align with ethical standards. This could involve implementing regulations, conducting audits, and promoting best practices in AI development and deployment.

Promoting digital literacy is another important strategy. By teaching people how to critically evaluate AI-generated content, recognize misinformation, and understand the limitations of AI, we can empower individuals to navigate the digital landscape responsibly. Collaboration between governments, tech companies, and civil society is also crucial in addressing these challenges. By working together, stakeholders can develop policies and initiatives that maximize the benefits of AI while minimizing its risks.

Virtual and Augmented Reality

Virtual reality (VR) and augmented reality (AR) are revolutionizing the way we communicate, offering immersive and interactive experiences that were once the stuff of science fiction. These technologies are transforming how people connect, share ideas, and collaborate, breaking down physical barriers and creating entirely new ways to interact with the world and each other. By blending the digital and physical realms, VR and AR are reshaping communication in education, healthcare, business, entertainment, and beyond, making it possible to experience and share ideas in ways that feel more real and engaging than ever before.

To understand the impact of VR and AR, it's important to first grasp what these technologies are and how they work. Virtual reality creates fully immersive digital environments that users can explore and interact with, often using VR headsets like the Oculus Quest or HTC Vive. When you put on a VR headset, you are transported to a completely different world—whether it's a virtual meeting room, a 3D recreation of ancient Rome, or a fantasy landscape. Everything you see and hear is generated by the VR system, making it feel as though you are truly present in that environment.

Augmented reality, on the other hand, overlays digital elements onto the real world, blending the physical and virtual. Unlike VR, AR does not replace your surroundings but enhances them with additional information or visuals. For example, AR applications like Pokémon GO allow users to see digital creatures superimposed on their real-world environment through their smartphone cameras. Similarly, AR glasses like Microsoft's HoloLens can project 3D models, instructions, or animations onto the user's field of view, creating a seamless mix of the real and the digital.

These technologies are not just about entertainment—they are transforming communication in profound ways. In education, for instance, VR and AR are creating immersive learning experiences that go far beyond traditional classrooms. Imagine a history class where students can step into a VR simulation of the Colosseum in ancient Rome, walking through its corridors and witnessing a gladiator fight as if they were there. Or consider an AR app that allows biology students to explore a 3D model of the human body, zooming in on organs and systems to understand how they work. These technologies make learning more engaging and interactive, helping students grasp complex concepts through hands-on experiences.

In healthcare, VR and AR are enhancing communication between doctors, patients, and medical teams. Surgeons can use AR abilities to overlay critical information, such as blood vessels or tumor locations, onto a patient's body during an operation, improving precision and outcomes. VR is also being used for medical training, allowing students to practice procedures in realistic virtual environments without the risks associated with real patients. For example, a trainee surgeon can perform a virtual operation using a VR system, gaining valuable experience and feedback before working in a real operating room. These technologies are not only improving skills but also fostering better communication and collaboration among medical professionals.

In the business world, VR and AR are enabling new ways of working and collaborating. Virtual reality platforms like Spatial and Horizon Workrooms allow teams to hold meetings in 3D virtual spaces, where participants can interact as avatars, share presentations, and brainstorm ideas as if they were in the same room. This is especially valuable for remote teams, as it creates a sense of presence and connection that video calls cannot replicate. Augmented reality is also being used in industries like manufacturing and retail, where workers can use AR glasses to access real-time instructions, troubleshoot equipment, or visualize product designs. These abilities streamline communication and make complex tasks easier to manage.

Entertainment is another area where VR and AR are transforming how people connect and share experiences. Virtual reality gaming has become increasingly popular, allowing players to step into immersive worlds and interact with others in real time. AR is enhancing live events, such as concerts and sports, by adding digital overlays that provide additional context or interactive elements. For example, fans at a soccer match can use an AR app to see player stats or replays projected onto their screens, enriching their experience and deepening their engagement.

While the opportunities offered by VR and AR are exciting, these technologies also come with challenges and limitations. One of the biggest barriers is cost. High-quality VR headsets and AR devices can be expensive, making them inaccessible to many people. This limits the widespread adoption of these technologies, particularly in developing countries or underserved communities. Additionally, the infrastructure required to support VR and AR, such as high-speed internet and powerful computing systems, is not yet universally available, further contributing to digital inequality.

Accessibility is another concern. Not everyone finds VR and AR experiences comfortable or easy to use. For example, some people experience motion sickness or eye strain when using VR headsets, while others may struggle with the technical skills required to operate these devices. Ensuring that these technologies are inclusive and user-friendly is essential for their long-term success.

Privacy and data security are also critical issues. VR and AR systems collect vast amounts of data about users, including their movements, preferences, and even physical environments. This raises concerns about how this data is stored, used, and protected. For example, an AR app that maps a user's surroundings could inadvertently capture sensitive information, such as the layout of their home. Ensuring that these technologies are designed with strong privacy protections is crucial to building trust and preventing misuse.

Finally, there are concerns about the psychological effects of spending extended periods in virtual environments. While VR and AR can create incredible experiences, they can also blur the line between reality and the digital world. Over-reliance on these technologies could lead to social isolation or a diminished appreciation for real-world interactions. Striking a balance between immersive digital experiences and meaningful real-world connections is essential to ensuring that these technologies enhance, rather than replace, human relationships.

Blockchain and Decentralized Networks

In a world where trust is often fragile and data breaches are increasingly common, blockchain technology and decentralized networks are transforming how we share, store, and secure information. By creating systems that are transparent, tamper-proof, and independent of centralized authorities, these technologies are ushering in a new era of trust and security. Blockchain, the foundation of decentralized networks, is not just a buzzword—it is a revolutionary way of ensuring that information is accurate, reliable, and accessible to all parties involved.

At its core, blockchain is a type of distributed ledger technology. Imagine a digital ledger, like a notebook, that records transactions or data entries. But instead of being stored in one place, this ledger is distributed across multiple computers, called nodes, around the world. Every time a new transaction is made, it is added to the ledger as a "block" of data. These blocks are linked together in chronological order, forming a "chain"—hence the name blockchain. What makes this system unique is that once a block is added to the chain, it cannot be altered or deleted. This immutability ensures that the data is secure and trustworthy.

To understand how blockchain works, let's use the example of cryptocurrency transactions, such as Bitcoin. When someone sends Bitcoin to another person, the transaction is broadcast to the entire network of nodes. These nodes work together to verify that the transaction is valid—for example, by checking that the sender has enough Bitcoin in their account. Once the transaction is verified, it is added to a block, which is then added to the blockchain. This process ensures that every transaction is transparent, secure, and recorded permanently.

Another powerful application of blockchain is smart contracts. A smart contract is a self-executing program that runs on the blockchain. It automatically enforces the terms of an agreement when certain conditions are met. For example, imagine a farmer and a buyer agree to a deal where the buyer will pay the farmer once a shipment of produce is delivered. A smart contract can be programmed to release the payment automatically when the shipment is confirmed, eliminating the need for intermediaries like banks or lawyers. This not only saves time and money but also ensures that the agreement is carried out fairly and transparently.

The benefits of blockchain and decentralized networks are far-reaching. One of the most significant advantages is enhanced security. Because the blockchain is distributed across many nodes, it is incredibly difficult for hackers to alter or manipulate the data. To successfully tamper with a blockchain, a hacker would need to gain control of more than half of the nodes in the network—a nearly impossible task for large, well-established blockchains like Bitcoin or Ethereum. This makes blockchain an ideal solution for storing sensitive information, such as financial records, medical data, or digital identities.

Transparency is another key benefit of blockchain. Every transaction or data entry on the blockchain is visible to all participants in the network. This openness fosters trust, as anyone can verify the accuracy of the information. For example, in supply chain management, blockchain can be used to track the journey of goods from the manufacturer to the consumer. A company can record every step of the process on the blockchain, ensuring that the products are authentic and ethically sourced. Consumers can then access this information to verify the origin and quality of the goods they purchase.

Blockchain also eliminates the need for intermediaries, streamlining processes and reducing costs. In traditional systems, intermediaries like banks, notaries, or brokers are often required to verify transactions or enforce agreements. Blockchain removes this need by providing a decentralized system where trust is built into the technology itself. This has led to the rise of decentralized finance (DeFi), where people can lend, borrow, or trade assets directly with one another without relying on banks or other financial institutions. DeFi platforms use blockchain to create a transparent and secure financial ecosystem that is accessible to anyone with an internet connection.

Digital identity is another area where blockchain is making a significant impact. Traditional identity systems, such as passports or driver's licenses, are often vulnerable to fraud or theft. Blockchain offers a solution by creating secure, tamper-proof digital identities that individuals can control. For example, a person's identity information can be stored on the blockchain, allowing them to prove their identity without sharing unnecessary personal details. This has applications in areas like voting, where blockchain can ensure that elections are secure and free from tampering.

Despite its many benefits, blockchain is not without challenges. One of the biggest issues is scalability. As more transactions are added to the blockchain, the size of the ledger grows, requiring more storage and processing power. This can slow down the network and make it less efficient, particularly for large-scale applications. Developers are working on solutions, such as sharding or layer-2 protocols, to address these scalability issues, but they remain a significant hurdle.

Another concern is the high energy consumption of some blockchain systems, particularly those that use proof-of-work (PoW) as their consensus mechanism. PoW requires nodes to solve complex mathematical problems to validate transactions, a process that consumes a large amount of electricity. For example, the

Bitcoin network has been criticized for its environmental impact, as its energy consumption rivals that of entire countries. Alternative consensus mechanisms, such as proof-of-stake (PoS), are being developed to reduce energy usage, but widespread adoption is still in progress.

Integrating blockchain into existing systems can also be complex and costly. Many organizations lack the technical expertise or resources to implement blockchain solutions, creating barriers to adoption. Additionally, the regulatory landscape for blockchain and cryptocurrencies is still evolving, with governments around the world grappling with how to regulate these technologies. Clear and consistent regulations are needed to provide legal certainty and encourage innovation while addressing concerns about misuse, such as money laundering or fraud.

Ethical Considerations in the Development of Future Technologies

As technology continues to evolve at an unprecedented pace, it is reshaping the way we live, work, and interact with the world. From artificial intelligence (AI) and genetic editing to autonomous vehicles and advanced surveillance systems, emerging technologies hold immense potential to improve lives and solve global challenges. However, with this potential comes great responsibility. The decisions made during the development and deployment of these technologies can have far-reaching consequences for individuals, societies, and the environment. This is why ethical considerations must be at the forefront of technology development, ensuring that innovation aligns with societal values and promotes the common good.

Ethics in technology development is about more than just avoiding harm—it is about actively designing systems that are fair, transparent, and accountable. Every new technology brings with it a set of ethical challenges that must be carefully addressed to prevent unintended consequences and ensure that the benefits are shared equitably. For example, AI systems, which are increasingly used in areas like hiring, policing, and healthcare, have the potential to perpetuate or even amplify biases present in the data they are trained on. If an AI system is trained on biased data, it may make decisions that unfairly disadvantage certain groups, such as women or minorities. This raises important questions about fairness and accountability: Who is responsible when an AI system makes a biased decision, and how can we ensure that these systems are designed to treat everyone equitably?

Privacy is another critical ethical consideration in the development of future technologies. As surveillance technologies become more advanced, the line between security and privacy becomes increasingly blurred. For example, facial recognition systems are now capable of identifying individuals in real time, raising concerns about how this data is collected, stored, and used. While these systems can be valuable for law enforcement or security purposes, they also pose significant risks to individual privacy and civil liberties. In some cases, governments or corporations may misuse these technologies to monitor citizens or suppress dissent, creating a chilling effect on freedom of expression. Balancing the benefits of surveillance with the need to protect privacy is a complex ethical challenge that requires careful consideration and regulation.

Autonomous vehicles present another set of ethical dilemmas, particularly in life-and-death scenarios. For instance, if a self-driving car is faced with an unavoidable accident, how should it decide whom to prioritize—the passengers in the car or pedestrians on the road? These decisions, often referred to as "trolley problems," highlight the difficulty of programming machines to make ethical choices in complex, real-world situations. Developers must grapple with questions about how to encode moral values into algorithms and who should be held accountable when things go wrong.

The potential for unintended consequences is another major ethical concern in technology development. Automation, for example, has the potential to displace millions of workers, particularly in industries like manufacturing, transportation, and retail. While automation can increase efficiency and reduce costs, it also raises questions about how to support workers whose jobs are replaced by machines. Similarly, technologies like deepfakes—AI-generated videos that can make it appear as though someone said or did something they never did—can be used to spread misinformation, manipulate public opinion, or damage reputations. These unintended consequences underscore the importance of anticipating and mitigating the risks associated with new technologies.

Genetic editing technologies, such as CRISPR, also raise profound ethical questions. While these technologies have the potential to cure genetic diseases and improve human health, they also open the door to controversial practices like "designer babies," where genetic traits are selected or modified for non-medical reasons. This raises concerns about equity, as access to genetic editing may be limited to the wealthy, exacerbating existing social and economic inequalities. It also raises questions about the long-term consequences of altering the human genome and the ethical boundaries of scientific experimentation.

Given these challenges, it is clear that developers, corporations, and governments have a shared responsibility to ensure that future technologies are designed and used responsibly. Developers must adopt an "ethics by design" approach, embedding ethical principles into the technology development process from the very beginning. This means considering the potential impacts of a technology on individuals and society, identifying risks, and taking steps to mitigate them. For example, developers of AI systems can conduct bias audits to ensure that their algorithms are fair and inclusive, or they can design systems that prioritize transparency, allowing users to understand how decisions are made.

Corporations also have a critical role to play in promoting ethical technology development. As the primary drivers of innovation, companies must prioritize ethical considerations alongside profitability. This includes being transparent about how their technologies work, engaging with diverse stakeholders to understand the potential impacts, and taking responsibility for the consequences of their products. For example, tech companies can establish ethics boards or advisory committees to provide guidance on complex ethical issues, or they can collaborate with researchers and policymakers to develop best practices for responsible innovation.

Governments, too, have a vital role in ensuring that technologies are developed and used in ways that align with societal values. This includes creating regulations and guidelines that promote transparency, accountability, and fairness. For example, governments can establish data protection laws to safeguard privacy, or they can require companies to conduct impact assessments before deploying new technologies. International collaboration is also essential, as many of the challenges associated with emerging technologies—such as cybersecurity threats or the misuse of AI—transcend national borders. Developing global frameworks and standards can help ensure that technologies are used responsibly and ethically on a global scale.

Inclusivity is another key principle in addressing ethical concerns. The development of future technologies should involve diverse perspectives, including those of marginalized communities, ethicists, and civil society organizations. This ensures that the voices of those who may be most affected by new technologies are heard and that the benefits are distributed equitably. For example, involving community representatives in the design of surveillance systems can help address concerns about privacy and discrimination, while engaging with ethicists can provide valuable insights into the moral implications of new technologies.

Chapter 13

Global Connectivity And The Flow of Ideas

The Promise of a Connected World

The world has never been more connected than it is today. Advancements in technology, the internet, and digital communication have created a global network where people can collaborate and innovate across industries, cultures, and borders. This connected world has unlocked unprecedented opportunities, allowing individuals and organizations to work together in real time, share ideas instantly, and pool resources to solve some of the world's most pressing challenges. The promise of a connected world lies in its ability to foster collaboration and spark innovation, creating a future where progress is driven by collective effort and shared knowledge.

One of the most transformative aspects of a connected world is the ability to collaborate without being limited by geographic location. The internet and digital platforms have made it possible for people to work together from anywhere in the world, breaking down barriers of distance and time. For example, remote work has become a standard practice in many industries, allowing teams to collaborate seamlessly across continents. Abilities like Zoom, Microsoft Teams, and Slack enable real-time communication and coordination, making it easier than ever for people to share ideas, solve problems, and achieve common goals.

Open-source projects are another powerful example of global collaboration. In open-source communities, developers from around the world contribute to building and improving software that is freely available to everyone. Projects like Linux, an open-source operating system, and the Python programming language have become essential abilities in technology and innovation, thanks to the collective efforts of thousands of contributors. These projects demonstrate how a connected world can harness the power of collaboration to create abilities and solutions that benefit everyone.

Global research collaborations have also accelerated progress in fields like science, medicine, and technology. The development of COVID-19 vaccines is a prime example of what can be achieved when the world comes together to address a common challenge. Scientists, researchers, and pharmaceutical companies from different countries worked together to share data, conduct trials, and develop vaccines in record time. This level of international cooperation would not have been possible without the connectivity provided by modern technology, which allowed researchers to exchange information and coordinate efforts on a global scale.

A connected world also fosters innovation by enabling the rapid exchange of ideas and access to diverse perspectives. When people from different backgrounds, cultures, and disciplines come together, they bring unique insights and approaches that can lead to groundbreaking solutions. For example, global tech hubs like Silicon Valley, Shenzhen, and Bangalore thrive because they attract talent from around the world, creating environments where diverse ideas can flourish. These hubs are hotbeds of innovation, driving advancements in areas like artificial intelligence, renewable energy, and biotechnology.

Crowdfunding platforms like Kickstarter and GoFundMe are another example of how connectivity drives innovation. These platforms allow creators, entrepreneurs, and innovators to pitch their ideas to a global audience and secure funding from supporters around the world. This has democratized access to resources, enabling individuals with great ideas but limited financial means to bring their projects to life. From innovative gadgets to groundbreaking films, crowdfunding has empowered countless creators to turn their visions into reality.

The benefits of a connected world extend beyond individual projects and industries. Connectivity has the potential to address global challenges, such as climate change, poverty, and public health crises, by enabling collaboration on a scale never seen before. For example, international organizations like the United Nations use digital platforms to coordinate efforts among member states, NGOs, and private companies, ensuring that resources and expertise are shared effectively. Similarly, initiatives like the Global Partnership for Education leverage connectivity to improve access to education in underserved regions, helping to bridge gaps in opportunity and knowledge.

However, the promise of a connected world is not without its challenges. One of the most significant issues is digital inequality— the gap between those who have access to technology and the internet and those who do not. While connectivity has created incredible opportunities for many, millions of people around the world still lack access to basic digital infrastructure. This digital divide disproportionately affects marginalized communities, rural areas, and developing countries, limiting their ability to participate in the benefits of a connected world. Addressing digital inequality is essential to ensuring that the opportunities created by connectivity are distributed equitably.

Cybersecurity threats are another major concern in a connected world. As more systems and devices become interconnected, the risk of cyberattacks increases. Hackers can exploit vulnerabilities in networks to steal sensitive information, disrupt services, or even compromise critical infrastructure. For example, ransomware attacks on hospitals or power grids can have devastating consequences, highlighting the need for robust cybersecurity measures to protect the systems that underpin our connected world.

Over-reliance on technology is another challenge that must be addressed. While digital abilities and platforms have made collaboration and innovation easier, they can also create dependencies that leave individuals and organizations vulnerable when systems fail. For example, a company that relies entirely on cloud-based abilities for its operations may face significant disruptions if those abilities go offline. Striking a balance between leveraging technology and maintaining resilience is crucial to ensuring that connectivity remains a strength rather than a weakness.

To fully realize the promise of a connected world, it is essential to address these challenges and ensure that collaboration and innovation are guided by ethical principles. This includes promoting inclusivity, so that everyone—regardless of their location or socioeconomic status—can benefit from connectivity. Governments, corporations, and civil society must work together to expand access to digital infrastructure, provide affordable devices, and invest in digital literacy programs that empower individuals to participate in the global network.

Transparency and accountability are also critical. As technology becomes more integrated into our lives, it is important to ensure that the systems and platforms we rely on are designed and used responsibly. This includes protecting user privacy, preventing the misuse of data, and ensuring that algorithms and decision-making processes are fair and unbiased. Collaboration between stakeholders is key to developing frameworks and standards that promote trust and safeguard the integrity of a connected world.

Addressing the Digital Divide

In today's world, access to digital technologies and the internet has become essential for education, work, healthcare, and even daily life. Yet, millions of people around the globe remain disconnected, unable to benefit from the opportunities that the digital age offers. This gap between those who have access to digital technologies and those who do not is known as the digital divide. It is a pressing issue that perpetuates inequality, limits opportunities, and excludes entire communities from participating fully in the modern world. Addressing the digital divide is not just about providing access to technology—it is about ensuring that everyone has the abilities, knowledge, and opportunities to thrive in an increasingly connected society.

The digital divide is caused by several factors, with economic disparities being one of the most significant. Many people, particularly in low-income households, cannot afford the devices or internet connections needed to access digital abilities. For example, a family struggling to make ends meet may not have the resources to buy a computer or pay for a reliable broadband connection. This lack of access creates a barrier to information, education, and economic opportunities, leaving these families at a disadvantage compared to those who can afford the technology.

Another major cause of the digital divide is the lack of infrastructure in rural or underserved areas. In many parts of the world, particularly in developing countries, internet access is limited or nonexistent because the necessary infrastructure, such as fiber-optic cables or cell towers, has not been built. Even in developed countries, rural communities often face slower internet speeds or higher costs compared to urban areas. This lack of infrastructure means that people living in these regions are cut off from the digital world, unable to access online education, telemedicine, or remote work opportunities.

Limited digital literacy is also a key factor contributing to the digital divide. Even when people have access to devices and the internet, they may not know how to use them effectively. For example, an older adult who has never used a smartphone or a computer may struggle to navigate online platforms or access important information. Similarly, individuals with low levels of education may find it difficult to use digital abilities, further widening the gap between those who can benefit from technology and those who cannot.

The consequences of the digital divide are far-reaching and deeply concerning. One of the most significant impacts is on education. During the COVID-19 pandemic, when schools around the world shifted to online learning, millions of students in remote or low-income areas were left behind because they lacked access to devices or the internet. For example, in some rural communities, students had to rely on printed worksheets or shared devices, making it nearly impossible to keep up with their peers who had access to high-speed internet and digital learning platforms. This educational gap not only affects students' academic performance but also limits their future opportunities, perpetuating cycles of poverty and inequality.

The digital divide also affects access to healthcare. Telemedicine, which allows patients to consult with doctors remotely, has become an important ability for providing healthcare in underserved areas. However, without internet access or digital literacy, many people cannot take advantage of these services. For example, a person living in a rural area without reliable internet may have to travel long distances to see a doctor, even for minor health issues that could be addressed through a virtual consultation. This lack of access to healthcare can have serious consequences for individuals and communities, particularly during public health crises.

Economic opportunities are another area where the digital divide has a significant impact. In today's digital economy, access to the internet is essential for finding jobs, starting businesses, and participating in e-commerce. For example, someone without internet access may struggle to apply for jobs, as many employers now require online applications. Similarly, small businesses in underserved areas may miss out on opportunities to reach customers online, limiting their growth and profitability. This exclusion from the digital economy not only affects individuals but also hinders economic development in entire regions.

Addressing the digital divide requires a multifaceted approach that tackles the root causes of the problem. One of the most important strategies is expanding broadband infrastructure to ensure that everyone, regardless of where they live, has access to reliable and affordable internet. Governments and private companies can work together to build the necessary infrastructure in rural and underserved areas, such as laying fiber-optic cables or deploying satellite internet. For example, initiatives like SpaceX's Starlink aim to provide high-speed internet to remote regions using satellite technology, helping to bridge the gap for communities that have been left behind.

Providing affordable devices is another critical step in addressing the digital divide. Programs that distribute low-cost laptops, tablets, or smartphones to low-income families can help ensure that everyone has the abilities they need to access the digital world. For example, initiatives like One Laptop Per Child have provided millions of children in developing countries with access to technology, enabling them to participate in digital learning and gain valuable skills.

Digital literacy programs are also essential for bridging the divide. These programs teach people how to use digital abilities and navigate the internet, empowering them to take advantage of the opportunities that technology offers. For example, community centers or libraries can offer free workshops on basic computer skills, helping older adults, low-income individuals, and other underserved groups build their confidence and competence in using technology.

Collaboration between governments, tech companies, and civil society is key to addressing the digital divide. Governments can implement policies and provide funding to support infrastructure development, device distribution, and digital literacy programs. Tech companies can play a role by designing affordable devices, offering low-cost internet plans, or partnering with nonprofits to reach underserved communities. Civil society organizations can advocate for digital inclusion, raise awareness about the issue, and provide on-the-ground support to those who need it most.

There are already many successful initiatives that demonstrate the power of collaboration in bridging the digital divide. For example, Google's Project Loon used high-altitude balloons to provide internet access to remote areas, while Microsoft's Airband Initiative works to bring broadband to underserved communities in the United States and around the world. Nonprofits like the Digital Divide Council and the Alliance for Affordable Internet are also working to promote digital inclusion and ensure that everyone has access to the abilities they need to succeed in the digital age.

The Role of Governments, Corporations, and Individuals in Shaping the Future

"The best way to predict the future is to create it." – Peter Drucker

The future is not something that simply happens to us—it is something we shape through our actions, decisions, and collaborations. Governments, corporations, and individuals each play a vital role in determining the direction of technology, society, and global progress. These three key stakeholders influence how we address challenges, seize opportunities, and build a world that reflects our shared values. By understanding their roles and responsibilities, we can work together to create a future that is sustainable, inclusive, and innovative.

Governments have a unique and powerful role in shaping the future. They set the rules and frameworks that guide society, create policies to address pressing issues, and invest in infrastructure and innovation to drive progress. Through regulations, governments ensure that new technologies are developed and used responsibly. For example, as artificial intelligence (AI) becomes more integrated into our lives, governments are working to create ethical guidelines and laws to prevent misuse, such as bias in AI systems or the spread of misinformation through deepfakes. These regulations help protect citizens while fostering trust in emerging technologies.

Governments also play a critical role in addressing global challenges like climate change. By promoting renewable energy and sustainable practices, they can lead the transition to a greener future. For instance, countries like Denmark and Germany have invested heavily in wind and solar energy, setting ambitious goals to reduce carbon emissions. These efforts not only combat climate change but also create jobs and stimulate economic growth in the renewable energy sector.

In addition to regulation and environmental initiatives, governments invest in education, healthcare, and infrastructure to ensure that their citizens have the abilities and opportunities to thrive. Programs that expand access to quality education, such as free public schooling or scholarships for higher education, empower individuals to contribute to society and the economy. Similarly, investments in healthcare systems ensure that people can live healthier, more productive lives. Governments also build and maintain infrastructure, such as roads, bridges, and internet networks, which are essential for connecting communities and enabling progress.

While governments set the stage, corporations are often the drivers of innovation and economic growth. Businesses develop new technologies, create jobs, and influence consumer behavior, shaping the way we live and work. Tech companies, for example, have revolutionized industries with advancements in artificial intelligence, renewable energy, and space exploration. Companies like Tesla have accelerated the adoption of electric vehicles, reducing reliance on fossil fuels and inspiring other automakers to follow suit. Similarly, SpaceX has made space exploration more accessible and cost-effective, opening up new possibilities for scientific discovery and commercial ventures.

Corporations also have a significant impact on society through their ethical responsibilities. As businesses grow and expand, they must consider the long-term effects of their actions on the environment, their employees, and the communities they serve. For example, many companies are adopting sustainable practices, such as reducing waste, using renewable energy, and creating eco-friendly products. These efforts not only benefit the planet but also appeal to consumers who prioritize sustainability in their purchasing decisions.

Data privacy is another area where corporations have a critical responsibility. In an age where personal information is collected and analyzed on an unprecedented scale, companies must ensure that data is handled securely and transparently. For instance, tech giants like Apple have emphasized user privacy by implementing features that give individuals more control over their data. By prioritizing ethical practices, corporations can build trust with their customers and contribute to a more equitable and secure digital landscape.

While governments and corporations play significant roles, individuals are the heart of shaping the future. Through collective action, consumer choices, and grassroots movements, people have the power to drive change and hold institutions accountable. Activism is one of the most visible ways individuals influence the future. For example, climate change advocacy led by figures like Greta Thunberg has inspired millions of people around the world to demand action from governments and corporations. These movements have pushed leaders to adopt more ambitious climate policies and invest in sustainable solutions.

Consumer choices also have a profound impact on shaping the future. When individuals choose to support businesses that align with their values—such as buying from companies that prioritize sustainability or ethical labor practices—they send a powerful message to the market. This demand for responsible products and services encourages corporations to adopt better practices and innovate in ways that benefit society.

Grassroots movements and social entrepreneurship are other ways individuals contribute to progress. Social entrepreneurs, for example, create businesses that address social or environmental challenges while generating economic value. Organizations like TOMS Shoes, which donates a pair of shoes for every pair sold, demonstrate how individuals can combine innovation with a commitment to making the world a better place. These efforts show that anyone, regardless of their background or resources, can play a role in shaping the future.

The most significant progress often comes when governments, corporations, and individuals work together. Collaboration is essential for addressing global challenges like climate change, inequality, and technological disruption. For example, the Paris Agreement on climate change brought together governments, businesses, and civil society to set goals for reducing carbon emissions and transitioning to renewable energy. This kind of partnership demonstrates the power of collective action in tackling complex issues that no single stakeholder can solve alone.

Shared responsibility and ethical decision-making are key to ensuring that the future is sustainable and inclusive. Governments must create policies that promote fairness and protect the public good. Corporations must prioritize ethical practices and long-term sustainability over short-term profits. Individuals must stay informed, make conscious choices, and hold institutions accountable. By working together, these three stakeholders can create a future that reflects our shared values and aspirations.

Building a More Inclusive and Transparent Information Network

In today's interconnected world, information networks are the backbone of how we communicate, learn, and make decisions. These networks—spanning the internet, social media platforms, search engines, and data-sharing systems—have the power to shape societies, influence economies, and connect people across the globe. However, the current state of information networks is far from perfect. Challenges such as digital inequality, algorithmic bias, misinformation, and a lack of transparency in how data is collected and used have created barriers that disproportionately affect marginalized communities and deepen social and economic disparities. To build a more inclusive and transparent information network, we must address these challenges and ensure that everyone has equitable access to technology, unbiased systems, and clear communication about how information is managed.

One of the most pressing issues in today's information networks is digital inequality. Millions of people around the world still lack access to the internet or the devices needed to participate in the digital age. This divide is often rooted in economic disparities, with low-income households unable to afford the necessary technology. It is also exacerbated by a lack of infrastructure in rural or underserved areas, where high-speed internet is unavailable or prohibitively expensive. Without access to information networks, individuals are excluded from opportunities in education, healthcare, and employment, perpetuating cycles of poverty and inequality.

Algorithmic bias is another significant challenge. Many of the systems that power information networks, such as search engines, recommendation algorithms, and artificial intelligence (AI), are designed using data that reflects existing societal biases. For example, an AI system used for hiring might favor candidates from certain demographics if the training data is skewed toward those groups. Similarly, search engines may prioritize content that reinforces stereotypes or excludes diverse perspectives. These biases can have real-world consequences, limiting opportunities for marginalized communities and perpetuating discrimination.

Misinformation is a growing problem in information networks, with false or misleading content spreading rapidly through social media and other platforms. This issue is often fueled by algorithms that prioritize engagement, amplifying sensational or emotionally charged content over accurate information. Misinformation can have serious consequences, from influencing elections to undermining public health efforts. For example, during the COVID-19 pandemic, false information about vaccines spread widely online, contributing to vaccine hesitancy and putting lives at risk.

A lack of transparency in how data is collected, shared, and used further complicates these challenges. Many users are unaware of how their personal information is being tracked and monetized by companies, leading to concerns about privacy and data security. For example, social media platforms often collect vast amounts of data about their users, but the processes behind this data collection are rarely explained in clear or accessible terms. This lack of transparency erodes trust in digital systems and leaves users vulnerable to exploitation.

To address these challenges, we must prioritize the principles of inclusivity and transparency in building information networks. Inclusivity means ensuring that everyone, regardless of their background or circumstances, has access to the abilities and opportunities provided by digital technologies. This includes expanding internet access in underserved areas, providing affordable devices, and implementing digital literacy programs to help people navigate the online world. For example, initiatives like Google's Project Loon, which uses high-altitude balloons to deliver internet to remote regions, demonstrate how technology can be used to bridge the digital divide.

Transparency, on the other hand, involves making information networks more open and accountable. This means designing systems that are easy to understand and providing clear explanations of how data is collected, shared, and used. Open-source platforms, where the underlying code is publicly available, are a great example of transparency in action. These platforms allow users to see how the system works and contribute to its development, fostering trust and collaboration. Community-driven initiatives, such as Wikipedia, also demonstrate the power of transparency by allowing users to verify and edit content collectively.

Governments, corporations, and civil society all have critical roles to play in building a more inclusive and transparent information network. Governments can create policies and regulations that promote digital inclusion and protect user privacy. For example, the European Union's General Data Protection Regulation (GDPR) sets strict guidelines for how companies handle personal data, giving users more control over their information. Governments can also invest in infrastructure projects to expand internet access and provide funding for digital literacy programs.

Corporations, as the creators and operators of many information networks, have a responsibility to design systems that are fair, accessible, and transparent. This includes addressing algorithmic bias by using diverse datasets and conducting regular audits to ensure fairness. Companies can also adopt ethical AI practices, such as prioritizing user privacy and avoiding the use of AI for harmful purposes. For example, Microsoft has committed to developing AI systems that are inclusive and accountable, setting an example for other tech companies to follow.

Civil society, including nonprofits, advocacy groups, and individual citizens, plays a vital role in holding governments and corporations accountable. Grassroots movements can raise awareness about digital inequality and push for policies that promote inclusivity. Nonprofits can provide digital literacy training and advocate for marginalized communities. For example, organizations like the Electronic Frontier Foundation work to protect digital rights and promote transparency in information networks.

Collaboration between these stakeholders is essential to creating a more inclusive and transparent information network. Governments, corporations, and civil society must work together to address the root causes of digital inequality, combat misinformation, and ensure that information networks are designed with fairness and accountability in mind. Public-private partnerships, such as those between tech companies and governments, can pool resources and expertise to tackle complex challenges. For example, partnerships to expand broadband access in rural areas have successfully connected millions of people to the internet.

The benefits of an inclusive and transparent information network are immense. By ensuring that everyone has access to digital technologies, we can empower individuals to participate fully in society and the economy. Transparent systems build trust, fostering collaboration and innovation. For example, open data initiatives, where governments and organizations share data publicly, have led to breakthroughs in areas like healthcare, urban planning, and environmental conservation. An inclusive and transparent information network also strengthens democracy by ensuring that citizens have access to accurate information and can hold institutions accountable.

However, building such a network is not without its challenges. Resistance to change, the cost of implementation, and the need for global cooperation can all pose obstacles. For example, expanding internet access in remote areas requires significant investment in infrastructure, while addressing algorithmic bias requires ongoing research and development. Overcoming these challenges will require sustained effort, collaboration, and a commitment to ethical principles.

www.ingramcontent.com/pod-product-compliance
Lightning Source LLC
LaVergne TN
LVHW051228050326
832903LV00028B/2299